Revised and Updated

The Ministry of Development™

An Introduction to
Stewardship and Development
for
Christian Ministries, Churches, and Non-Profit Organizations

With New Material on:

Stewardship as a Lifestyle

D1483719

Dr. John R. Frank, CFRE

With an Introduction by

Larry F. Johnston, Ph.D.

Mennonite Church Canada
Resource Centre
600 Shaftesbury Blvd., Winnipeg, MB R3P 0M4
Toll-free: 1-866-888-6785

© 2010 John R. Frank and Steward Publishing
All Rights Reserved.

No part of this publication may be reproduced, stored in a retrieval system, or
transmitted, in any form or by any means, electronic, mechanical, photocopying,
recording, or otherwise, without the written permission of the author.

Dog Ear Publishing
4010 W. 86th Street, Ste H
Indianapolis, IN 46268
www.dogearpublishing.net

ISBN: 978-160844-652-0

This book is printed on acid-free paper.

Printed in the United States of America

The Ministry of Development
Copyright © 1995 by John R. Frank
All rights reserved.
ISBN - 978-0-9754399-0-6

8000 printed to date — 1995

Revised and Updated - 2010 by Design Group International™
P.O. Box 19
Kohler, WI 53044
www.DesignGroupInternational.com

All scripture quotations are taken from the HOLY BIBLE,
NEW INTERNATIONAL VERSION. Copyright © 1973, 1978, 1984 by
the International Bible Society.

the Revised Edition

When the book first was published in 1995, I was happy simply to have it completed. Since then I have been thankful and in awe of how God used it. At a conference in Los Angeles a man walked up to me and said, "I was ready to quit. This raising of money is not for me. Then I read your book and realized it was not my job to raise money. It was God's job to move through his people to give."

Another time a man came and told me he had read my book for the third time. And for the third time he learned something to help him in his ministry. I was recently at a book signing with someone who had just written a book on relationships in stewardship. As we got acquainted he said that my book was the first every member of his organization's development department had to read. It was considered their best intro to development for any nonprofit ministry.

Over time , most books should are in used bookstores and new ones replace them. I do not take personal pride in great writing skill, Rather, I am amazed and humbled at how God used this small book, perhaps because it grows from God's Word.

The truth and impact of this book is in the first chapter's heading – Is Development part of God's plan? All that follows builds upon a resounding "Yes" to that question.

As the years pass I work more and more in the area of Biblical stewardship. The perspective I have gained is reflected in some of the added chapters in this book. They are formed from my experience and doctoral dissertation developed for my Doctor of Ministry in Leadership for the Emerging Culture, from George Fox Evangelical Seminary.

I want to thank again the people at Saint Mary's University's Philanthropy and Development program. They continue to offer program and provide impact for the stewardship and development community. One of my mentors when I first developed this book, Tim Burchill, recently passed away unexpectedly. He was one of the founders of the program and a personal help to me in writing this book. He is greatly missed.

My prayer is that this small book will continue to be used by people new to the ministry of development, board members, those moving from philanthropy to stewardship, and pastors. May we all look more closely at what stewardship and development can and should be.

Original Acknowledgments

As with any undertaking, I am aware of and grateful for the many people who have helped make this project a reality.

First, I must thank my classmates in the Master of Arts in Philanthropy and Development program from Saint Mary's University of Minnesota. Without their encouragement and support at a critical time in my career, this book would not have been possible. They are all special people, and the time with them during our M.A. program was rewarding.

My thanks also go to Tim Burchill, CFRE, my faculty advisor. His excellent editing and timely encouragement were instrumental in the completion and quality of this book.

Dr. Bob Moorehead served as my on-site resource person for this project; my thanks to him for his patient reading and rereading of the drafts. I am thankful for the time he took to encourage me as a new writer.

Rachel Derowitsch provided much needed and appreciated editing and guidance. My thanks to her.

There are not enough words to thank my wife, Susan. She is my best friend and constant listener and encourager. Without her I would not be where I am now. I am so thankful for the wife God has given me.

Kyle and Sarah put up with Dad being locked away in his home office. Thanks to them for putting up with my long trips away from home.

Thanks also to my mom and dad for their constant support and encouragement.

And finally, I am thankful for Jesus Christ. My relationship with him has brought purpose to my life and a calling in this area of ministry. To him be the glory.

Original Foreword

This book has been a goal and dream of mine for some time, springing out of my varied experiences in development. As with any effort this large, a catalyst for starting and staying on task is needed. The Master of Arts in Philanthropy and Development from Saint Mary's University of Minnesota proved to be exactly that—a catalyst in my life.

This program was so invigorating, challenging and fun I found it difficult to consider it completed. This work was written as my Project Demonstrating Mastery. I received encouragement and support throughout the process and am thankful for this opportunity to share my thoughts, concerns, theories and techniques.

My purpose for this book is to add something helpful to the field of Christian development, which I truly love and feel a calling to. I hope it proves to be a foundation upon which quality, God-honoring development is built in many ministries.

The first portion of the book lays the scriptural foundations for development as a ministry. This includes bible references as well as my related definitions and theories.

The second portion stresses the technical applications of a development effort within a Christian ministry. General principles as well as some proven, specific strategies are given. This section shows how to implement a development ministry philosophy.

During my 15 of years of working in parachurch ministries as a staff member and now as a consultant to ministries, I have been enthused and excited by the ministry of development. There is so much potential to involve God's people in his great plan for all people.

And yet there is so much disparity in the quality and philosophies of development programs in ministries today. Some people believe it is best only to pray and wait for God to supply. Others try every fund- raising technique found in the latest magazines or how-to seminars.

Christian ministries need to become grounded in the "whys" of development. Why do we raise funds? Why does God desire stewardship? Why do we need development? Why do donors need to give?

My desire is to offer a foundation to Christian development. My hope and prayer is that whether you are a new development professional, a board member or a seasoned veteran, you will find this information relevant, encouraging, challenging and usable.

If we as professional development officers in Christian ministries can build our programs on biblical principles, there is no end to the opportunities to see God use his people to change lives—both now and for eternity.

I am thankful for the opportunity to offer this book and pray it will be used to bring glory to God through its reading and implementation.

— John R. Frank

Table of Contents

SECTION THREE
Implementation of a Ministry of Development Philosophy

Introduction

Larry F. Johnston
President, McConkey/Johnston, Inc.

Development.

The word appears in a hundred different contexts every day. Real estate development. Human resource development. Management and staff development. Personal development. Psychological development. Physical development. Economic development.

Yet for those involved in the field of philanthropy, development will typical take on one of two meanings. For neophytes — and those who see the field only through very narrow lenses — development is often a euphemism for fundraising. Unsure of the status of their profession, "development" is a face-saving semantic sidestep, a way of saying what you do without having to say what you really do —that is, raising funds.

For the true professional, however, development encompasses much more than fundraising although resource mobilization will always be at the core of development. For the real professionals, and John Frank is clearly one of them, development is a comprehensive set of more than 30 distinct disciplines ranging from strategic planning to persuasion theory, from human resource development to charitable estate planning, and from information systems to direct response advertising.

Regardless of the definition you choose, development — or, in a larger sense philanthropy and institutional advancement — is BIG business. While private enterprise and government comprise the two main sectors of the American economy, the "third sector" of philanthropy is now responsible for a whopping total of more than $125 billion annually. No small chuck of cash by any measurement.

"If you think education is expensive, you should consider the cost of ignorance."

As with other professions, development has become a highly sophisticated blend of disciplines that can demand rigorous study and exacting skills. The fact that a number of institutions of higher education now offer masters and doctorates in the field is testimony to how far the profession of development has come in recent years.

Yet while sophistication and complexity in development proliferate at a mind-numbing pace, at its core, development is simple. *It is people helping people.*

And whether that help comes in rehabilitative services to a handicapped child, scholarships for deserving student, or emergency relief and humanitarian services to victims of floods, earthquakes, or tornadoes, the unsung heroes of development will always be behind the scenes. It is often their vision, their relentless dissatisfaction with the status quo, their compassion and their passion, their strategic thinking and resource development programs — along with board members, staff, and countless thousands of volunteers — that connect a vast array of human needs with the resources essential to meeting them.

But because philanthropy is both big business and, more important, something that helps make us truly human, development like brain surgery, should not be left to amateurs. The price, in terms of needs unmet, is simply too high.

More important, however, than the mere "how tos," board members, chief executives, development staff and volunteers need to understand the "why tos." Rather than becoming ruthless pragmatists or technicians skilled at anesthetizing donors before surgically separating them from their assets, those in development must understand that theirs is high calling. They must understand that,

> Vision, without development, is merely visionary.
> Development, without vision, is mercenary.
> Yet development, with vision, is missionary.

That's why John Frank's book, The *Ministry of Development* remains both important and timely. In it he puts forth the biblical reasons for giving and thereby establishes a foundation for development that rests on the Highest Authority. But because John is a savvy and seasoned veteran of development wars in addition to being a committed Christian, he knows that "God talk" alone won't make it in today's highly demanding and competitive field of development. That's why his simple and straightforward presentation of development philosophy, principles, basic concepts and guidelines is so worthwhile.

The great poet William Butler Years once said that "Education is not the filling of a pail, but the lighting of a fire." It is my hope that the pages that follow, rather than merely filling the reader's mind with thoughts, will spark a fire of serious reflection on the foundational issues of development. If this book succeeds in doing only that, it will have fulfilled a vital purpose.

- Larry F. Johnston

Publisher's Note

Design Group International™ is honored to publish this revised and expanded edition of *The Ministry of Development*. This little volume has been pressed into the hand of many a new development officer for Christian ministry organizations in Canada and the United States, heading off many potential problems because they followed its advice.

Dr. John Frank continues his helpfulness by updating and adding to the material so that a new generation of those raising support for ministry will be helped.

Go ahead and highlight the text. Write your notes in the margins. Dog-ear the pages. Buy extras to hand to your colleagues and to give to your advisory committees. Send people links to download this book to their e-readers. Find myriad ways to put this wisdom to work.

We won't mind.

Mark L. Vincent, Ph.D., CSP
CEO, Design Group International™

SECTION ONE

The Philosophy of a
Ministry of Development

CHAPTER ONE

Is Development Part of God's Plan?

The question is a fair one. Do we believe the profession of raising funds for Christian ministries, the local church, and other nonprofit organizations pleases God and is something in which he wants his people to be actively involved? Is development more than just the end result—having more funds?

I offer the definition of Christian development as *connecting God's people to God's work*. This process of creating opportunities to link people who believe in God and his kingdom work on earth, with the work itself, is development. This connection might take the form of prayers, time and gifts of money.

A key component of this connection is relationships. God is God over our relationships. Nothing matters more to him. It is within relationships that everything important in life is accomplished. This is true of stewardship and development. Development is building a relationship with people and the causes they care about. The gift is only a component of that relationship.

Consistent with this definition, I believe development is an integral part of God's plan—even more so today due to the proliferation of Christian nonprofit organizations that are local, regional, national and international in scope. The work of the Gospel has expanded to include numerous types of nonprofit ministries with various sizes of budgets and programs.

Each ministry must examine itself and ask, Are we raising funds only to have more money to "do ministry"? Or do we believe there is more to development than the techniques of acquiring more dollars? An organization's motivation will reveal which definitions, theories and, ultimately, which techniques are used in every development department. This issue of motivation will be examined in more detail later.

Defining development as a *process* of involving people in the actual work of the ministry rather than only the end result (needed funds) is important to the consideration of development as a ministry. We see throughout scripture that God involves people in the process. When Moses led the Israelites out of Egypt, they were not whisked away on a magic carpet to the promised land. God could have done that—He had been doing other miracles through Moses. Instead, He chose to take the Israelites through the *process* of finding freedom from slavery.

Involving donors in the ministry can happen in a number of ways. One international music ministry asked donors to send young people on a ministry tour to another country. It trained the young musicians to create a team of people who would pray for them, give to their support account and receive their ministry reports along the way. Though the supporters could not go on the tour, they became a part of the musical ministry through their giving.

Our culture wants end results fast. Development programs and marketing track statistics and success. Results motivate most executive staffs today. But is our obsession with end results pleasing to God? The process of involving God's people in the work of the ministry through prayer, giving and volunteering *is as important to the people who give as it is to the organization that receives*—in some ways maybe more important.

This involvement is living a stewardship lifestyle, one in which giving is an outgrowth of our relationship with Jesus Christ.

This stewardship of time, resources and prayers is at the core of who we are as Christians. The relationship between stewardship, development and philanthropy will be discussed in more detail later.

A multitude of ministries
Each Christian organization has at its foundation a cause, calling or special purpose. The founder of such an organization feels strongly that his or her ministry is part of God's plan.

The evangelistic outreach organization follows a calling to take the message of the Gospel to foreign countries, to the inner cities or to the television airwaves.

The Christian educator senses a deep commitment to follow God's plan by establishing a school in which every facet, from board members to curriculum to athletics, is connected to the purpose of the school under God.

Yet in each of these thousands of organizations the question arises, how do we find/raise the money needed to carry on the work?

God is our source
God is our source for everything. God is our creator and has creation at his disposal. One would have trouble arguing with the fact that God could, in a single gift, provide all the necessary funding to preach the Gospel, feed the hungry and teach the children . Yet God does not.. At least, not through our way of looking at it. God tends to work through stewards to achieve these goals.

Partners and stakeholders
What God does is enable us to work through organizations. Working through organizations includes funding the work. And when we provide funds for the work we are joining with the ministry. We become partners and stakeholders in the work to which we give.

Stewardship has taken on a more holistic definition, including the giving of one's time and talent. More and more organizations offer opportunities for people to "roll up their sleeves" and work themselves.

In the next few chapters I will examine God's plan to use development to involve his people in this work. To lead and motivate people to feed the hungry, teach the children, share the Gospel or hire a pastor is a critical part of our relationship with Jesus Christ. So it follows that as donors give to these causes, their giving is a part of their relationship with God.

Giving is a reflection of our relationship with Jesus Christ
Through this maturing relationship we see how our giving mirrors God's giving. Our spirit of giving (and therefore each donor's) is carried through to each act of mercy, kindness and love that our ministries perform. Just as Christ made the ultimate sacrifice for us, God desires that we learn to be givers in our everyday lives in response to his generosity.

With Jesus as our model of personal generosity, we can see that stewardship and giving is a component of discipleship, a way of following Christ.

The Ministry of Development

God's People → Development → Ministry

Development is creating opportunities for God's people to invest in God's work.

Figure 1

God uses development in the lives of donors and the organization

Development is a catalyst for connecting God's people to the ministries they love and care about. And through their giving they experience the joy and fulfillment of obeying God and seeing lives changed.

The organization, then, benefits from increased funding, but more important are the partnerships, prayers and increased awareness of the needs and results of the ministry—a greater overall support that donors give to the organization.

An elderly woman named Mary called concerning the public announcement of the Union Gospel Mission of Seattle's capital campaign. We were well past 50 percent of the goal and had sent a mailing to our list of supporters. She said she was on a fixed income and did not understand what this campaign was about.

I thanked her for her call and explained the campaign, the projects and our progress. I also let her know her previous support was appreciated and with her fixed income she need not worry about the campaign. She asked again about the projects and how the children would benefit.

She then said she wanted to pledge to the campaign. I was hesitant to see her do this and reminded her of her fixed income and how her current giving was doing a great work. I have never forgotten her response: "No, this is important. I'll just have to cut something else out."

Mary's desire to serve God through giving could not be thwarted. She knew she needed to give to meet her calling, not the organization's.

These increased and improved relationships with donors and friends of an organization have the greatest long-term impact on the cause. The more that development creates opportunities for God's people to be connected to God's work, the more work can be done.

Is development part of God's plan? Yes! From the founding vision, to the creation of programs, to the development efforts that involve God's people in giving, praying and volunteering, each and every aspect of this process is a part of God's plan for his people and his work.

CHAPTER TWO

Scriptural Foundations for Giving

The basis of understanding and developing the theory that development is a ministry is in its adherence to scripture. If we cannot show that the principles of giving, sharing, investing in and caring for God's work and God's people are consistent with scripture, then there is no basis for claiming the work of development is ministry.

The following general concepts with corresponding scripture provide a starting place for what should be a lifetime of examining God's Word in light of the profession of development.

1. Our attitude toward possessions

"The earth is the Lord's, and everything in it, the world, and all who live in it" (Psalm 24:1).

"And my God will meet all your needs according to his glorious riches in Christ Jesus" (Philippians 4:19).

"The land must not be sold permanently, because the land is mine and you are but aliens and my tenants" (Leviticus 25:23).

"But who am I, and who are my people, that we should be able to give as generously as this? Everything comes from you, and we have given you only what comes from your hand" (1 Chronicles 29:14).

"For the world is mine, and all that is in it" (Psalm 50:12).

These verses give us a picture of how God wants us to look at what we "own". Do we truly see ourselves as stewards, managers and caretakers of God's creation? Or do we seek to accumulate and desire the newest and the best? Having nice things is not against God's Word, but making them idols or placing them above our love for and obedience to God is.

It is critical that development officers embrace this understanding of ownership—a key principle of stewardship—before we share it with our donors.

Finding a donor who recognizes this principle is exciting. He or she will commonly say, "I'm just taking care of what God has given to me. I feel compelled to give back to God what he already owns."

At the foundation of this premise is a belief that God owns everything. We own nothing. Our jobs, houses, children, health and the blood that runs through our veins are all made by God, and God alone has authority over them.

Yet God gives us freedom to use or misuse all of creation. This point of ownership is critical, yet elusive. God owns creation as its Author, yet God gives us control, or a type of ownership over our health and wealth and our use of them.

In this discussion we are not exploring the subject of God's will and our free will. Suffice it to say, God gives us a great deal of choice in how we look at what we have been given and what we do with it. This understanding is the source for the principle of stewardship. Wesley K. Willmer, one-time chair of the Board of the Christian Stewardship Association, wrote in the 1993-94 *CSA Courier*, *"Stewardship is a way of looking at life and, more importantly, a way of living as a Christian in a non-Christian world. Christian stewardship is God's order for humanity's relationship to God, not humanity's relationship to an organization."*

What does the world apart from Christian beliefs or values hold as guiding principles regarding possessions? One finds multiple beliefs.

First is a greed mentality. You go around only once, so get all you can. Take it from someone else or they will take it from you. Make all you can, save all you can and accumulate. Greed is superficial and materialistic. We see it depicted on TV and in movies. Even though greed is often portrayed as evil I wonder how many viewers think, *I should have that kind of life. I deserve it.* Studies of social trends show that a growing number of young people agree with the greed philosophy. From buying patterns to the rising concern over personal credit card debt, the current and upcoming generation clearing embraces a "have it all now mentality."

We have seen an generations that left the church in their young adult years return with their families because of their spiritual needs. They have not received any training in stewardship, possessions or materialism from the church, but they have received much training from the world during this time. It is common to see a "What's in it for me?" mentality prevalent in churches today.

Another belief regarding possessions is more moderate. It is the acceptance of God as Creator and the view of humans as consumers. In other words, respect the manufacturer but hoard all products. "I believe God made these things, but they are for me to enjoy. Anything I earn is mine."

There is a "playing both sides" mentality here. Many Christians find this level comfortable. They enjoy accumulating good things and give of their "surplus" as it is comfortable. They give to God as if they are doing God a favor.

A belief more in tune with God's heart is the acknowledgment of God as the Creator and Supplier, and an obedience to his teaching on how these blessings should be cared for, grown and used. This philosophy understands that *everything* is temporal. As individuals and as nations, we have been given much in terms of possessions and resources, but they will one day fade away. How we manage every one of these things is important to God. This kind of stewardship brings a peace and joy to believers. They know there are no shortages in God's plan. They see the world through a filter of managing what has been given to them.

This belief that God created a shared ownership of resources and organizations is critical to all other scriptural concepts. The related points of this book that follow all have at their foundation this concept: *everything belongs to God in the first place, and God shall supply each of us with resources.* There is no shortage with God.

2. Why give?

Motivation for giving is a subject of much study and many theories. For the believer it is clearly spelled out in God's Word. Above all the scriptural principles about giving, God wants us to understand this: giving is important to him and he desires obedience.

"Honor the Lord with your wealth, with the first fruits of all your crops" (Proverbs 3:9).

Why give? Because God commanded and asked us to. Yes, both.

In the Old Testament, giving was commanded within specific guidelines. In the New Testament, we are given directions in how we should give, but with a new attitude—one of freedom and love for giving because of our relationship with Jesus Christ. We have directions for giving not because God "needs" our gifts, but because God wants to teach us to become givers.

"Each of you must bring a gift in proportion to the way the Lord your God has blessed you" (Deuteronomy 16:17).

The Old Testament gives us many guidelines that are still applicable today. In Deuteronomy we see an important principle for giving and for development in general: Give in proportion to how you have been given releases the development officer from thinking that God expects the same from everyone. It shows that each person or family has a responsibility to give according to THEIR ability, not in relationship to others or to development programs.

The important point to notice is that people give at various levels based on what they have. This translates to the donor pyramid of giving used by many churches and nonprofit organizations. This will be discussed in a later chapter.

"On the first day of every week, each one of you should set aside a sum of money in keeping with his income, saving it up, so that when I come no collections will have to be made" (1 Corinthians 16:2).

Giving on the first day of the week corresponded to when people in that day were paid and when they worshipped. Today, we all have various times and methods for receiving paychecks. The principle to be learned is to discipline oneself to give on a regular basis and in the context of a worshipping community.

The follow-up to this point is to give *first* to God. God seeks our firstfruits, not because God needs them, but because it is a demonstration of our belief that the best should go to God—the cream of the crop—as well as an acknowledgment of God's ownership. This is a tough one for many people to understand and accept. "Doesn't God want me to pay my bills first?" "Isn't it important to care for my spouse and children first?" "Isn't this part of being a good witness?"

If we accept the earlier point of God taking care of all our needs, we must fight the idea that if we do not pay our bills first, our family will starve and we will be on the street. God wants us to give to him first, plain and simple. Might the giving of gifts and the paying of bills be managed in such a way as to give a number of times rather than all out of one check? Yes, this is acceptable. But regardless of when we tithe and pay our bills, I believe God wants us to write the check to the Lord's work first.

I have experienced this on several occasions. One in particular was when I was a new teacher (earning a low salary) and I had to make a deposit for my place on a summer missions trip. It had to be in by December. With my rent, bills and expected Christmas gifts, I would not have enough to make the gift for my ministry trip. I prayed about it and sent the check. No, I didn't receive a check in the mail for the same amount. But I did have enough to pay my bills and buy my Christmas gifts. God supplied my needs through unexpected gifts and careful money management.

When I had a serious illness and was out of work for two months, we (my pregnant wife and two-year-old son) used up all of our savings, sick leave and vacation time. But during that time we did not stop giving to the church, the missionaries we supported and other ministries. We felt they needed our promised support. God healed me, took care of my family and taught my wife and me a valuable lesson in trusting God. This is not to imply that this is the same course everyone should follow. But we knew it was right for us to do.

Giving first shows the attitude of our hearts, that this is God's and God has asked us to give our firstfruits, our best. This is how to demonstrate that—by giving to God's work first. This is not easy and it may take time to develop. But once it is done it becomes an integral part of an ongoing and vibrant relationship with God.

Evangelist Billy Graham wrote in a *Seattle Post-Intelligencer* column, "*The important thing is not the amount of money you give. The important thing is the attitude of the heart. We should give, you see, not to earn God's favor or to pay him back somehow for what He has done for us, but because we love him."*

3. Attitude toward giving

Does it matter to God what a donor thinks or feels when he gives a gift? Yes! This a very important aspect of our relationship with God.

I have witnessed many offerings in churches after someone in leadership tells a joke and follows it by paraphrasing 2 Corinthians 9:7: "Let's all be cheerful when we give"—as if we should have a good sense of humor about it. But I believe God considers more than our humor when we give. God really does want us to give with a joy and excitement as we understand how giving is a part of God's relationship with us as believers.

"Freely you have received, freely give" (Matthew 10:8).

Giving our gifts each week or month to our church and charities should come from a free choice. This is a new freedom demonstrated in New Testament giving. Just as in Christ we have a new freedom from the Law, likewise we have a freedom to give liberally, without rules and regulations outlined in the Old Testament.

"Each man should give what he has decided in his heart to give, not reluctantly or under compulsion, for God loves a cheerful giver" (2 Corinthians 9:7).

In his second letter to the Corinthians, Paul makes it perfectly clear that God is concerned with the attitude of our heart when we give. We should not have to be manipulated or coerced. A *free* gift is one that truly pleases God. This is also true in our ministry of development. When an organization receives a gift from a donor who has given just for the sake of giving and without any conditions or restrictions, it is a joyful experience.

Promises regarding giving

Many churches and nonprofit groups shy away from the subject of what God promises us when we give. They do not want to appear as prosperity preachers or get investigated by *60 Minutes*. But the truth from God's Word is that God makes many promises to those who give to God and his work.

These blessings from God cover a variety of areas, including health, refreshment and taking care of our needs. Of special note is Philippians 4:17, which suggests that God indeed does see what we give and keeps track!

"Not that I (Paul) am looking for a gift, but I am looking for what may be credited to your account" (Philippians 4:17).

"Honor the Lord with your wealth, with the first fruits of all your crops; then your barns will be filled to overflowing, and your vats will brim over with new wine" (Proverbs 3:9–10).

"A generous man will prosper; he who refreshes others will himself be refreshed" (Proverbs 11:25).

"A generous man will himself be blessed, for he shares his food with the poor" (Proverbs 22:9).

As we examine these and other scripture passages, we see God's promises that those who give will receive. In our society this smacks of hucksterism. "Give so you can get" can be heard behind appeals from some religious fund-raisers. But there remains some truth to this principle of receiving something when we give—and sometimes more than what we give.

In his book *Give to Live*, Doug Lawson, Ph.D., suggests this and even more. His research indicates that people can live longer and healthier lives as a result of giving. He states that there are physical, emotional and spiritual benefits to giving, such as *"reducing the emotional stress that interferes with the body's self-maintenance system"*, and *"creating a stronger self-image."* (p.24-31).

What does God say? A generous man will be blessed. But how? Could it be with peace of mind? A knowledge of helping someone? Peace from knowing you are obedient to God? Good health? Wisdom in times of stress? Trusting that God will supply your needs, even material needs?

"Bring the whole tithe into the storehouse, that there may be food in my house. 'Test me in this,' says the Lord Almighty, 'and see if I will not throw open the floodgates of heaven and pour out so much blessing that you will not have room enough for it" (Malachi 3:10).

"Give, and it will be given to you. A good measure, pressed down, shaken together and running over, will be poured into your lap. For with the measure you use, it will be measured to you" (Luke 6:38).

The above verses point out two critical sections of scripture. Both present the case that God is prepared to bless those who give. God tells Malachi that the Israelites are robbing him and suggests they test him to see if his Word is true and that he will supply their needs.

Jesus uses the opportunity in the Luke passage to teach a number of concepts about how we should live our lives. Chief among them is this: learn to be a giver, and you will see your gifts multiplied back in your life beyond what you could ever give.

4.   What should I give?
Sometimes we look for opportunities to involve donors in ways other than financial gifts. Other times donors look for ways to "get out of" giving a gift of cash. Does one take the place of the other? Can we give time instead of cash? The following scriptures show the variety of tangible ways we can give to one another and therefore to God.

Clothing. *"I needed clothes and you clothed me"* (Matthew 25:36).

"What good is it, my brothers, if a man claims to have faith but has no deeds? Can such faith save him? Suppose a brother or sister is without clothes and daily food. If one of you says to him, 'Go, I wish you well; keep warm and well fed,' but does nothing about his physical needs, what good is it? In the same way, faith by itself, if it is not accompanied by action, is dead" (James 2:14–17).

Food and drink. *"For I was hungry and you gave me something to eat, I was thirsty and you gave me something to drink, I was a stranger and you invited me in"* (Matthew 25:35).

Hospitality. *"Share with God's people who are in need. Practice hospitality"* (Romans 12:13).

Medicine and time. *"I was sick and you looked after me, I was in prison and you came to visit me"* (Matthew 25:36).

Money. *"Jesus sat down opposite the place where the offerings were put and watched the crowd putting their money into the temple treasury. Many rich people threw in large amounts. But a poor widow came and put in two very small copper coins worth only a fraction of a penny. Calling his disciples to him, Jesus said, 'I tell you the truth, this poor widow has put more into the treasury than all the others. They all gave out of their wealth; but she, out of her poverty, put in everything— all she had to live on'"* (Mark 12:41-44).

Skills and talents. *"We have different gifts, according to the grace given us. If a man's gift is prophesying, let him use it in proportion to his faith. If it is serving, let him serve; if it teaching, let him teach; if it is encouraging, let him encourage; if it is contributing to the needs of other, let him give generously; if it is leadership, let him govern diligently, if it is showing mercy, let him do it cheerfully"* (Romans 12:6-8).

As we see by these examples, one type of giving does not take the place of the other. We are to be givers of our time, talents *and* treasure. We should be ready to share our clothing, medicine and our homes with those in need.

It is understandable that we cannot open our home to every homeless person we come across. But we can provide for the homeless by giving to a local church or mission that opens its doors for emergency housing. This does not excuse us, however, from providing a room, a bed, or sometimes our homes, to those we know are in need.

To summarize: scripture lists a variety of ways in which we can share what we have with those in need. We are also to give in *all* areas, including financial. Volunteering, while a generous gift of time, does not excuse anyone from also giving money.

We should also be aware that each type of giving might come in seasons. There are seasons in our lives where we have more time to give than money. Likewise, there are seasons where we have more income to give larger gifts than we have time to volunteer. But nowhere does scripture say we should not give anything. We are always to be givers in some way or another.

5.   Old Testament teaching on giving
There are numerous examples of giving and teaching on giving in the Old Testament. From Moses to Malachi we see how Almighty God is very concerned with how people give - to God, and to each other.

One example applicable even today concerns David. In 1 Chronicles 29 King David and the Israelites gave so that the temple could be built to house the tabernacle. This was an important capital campaign, and David followed a strategy consistent with today's campaign strategies.

First, David gave his own sacrificial gift. Then he asked his leaders to give. Then he went to the people. Through this process the campaign was successful, the people were enthusiastic givers, and the work was completed. Most importantly, God was honored through the entire process.

6. New Testament teaching on giving

Richard Perry, partner in the Domain Group, writes in his booklet, *A Biblical Look at Fund Raising*, *"Fund raising is the ministry of encouraging the grace of giving."* He goes on to point out how Jesus was donor-driven in his teaching about the man who wanted to inherit eternal life. Jesus directed him to sell all he had and give to the poor—a sacrificial gift to say the least. Jesus also shows us the widow who gave a small gift that was great in relation to her entire giving ability. Jesus was concerned not with the gifts in either instance, but with the salvation of the man and the heart of the widow. Jesus' concern for the person as opposed to the gift is a perfect example of being donor-driven.

The apostle Paul carried on the teachings of Jesus about giving. 2 Corinthians 8 and 9 give a clear picture of New Testament giving. Paul writes to the Corinthians on a number of issues related to financial needs, attitudes toward giving and how God looks at giving.

Of special note here is how Paul refers to the *"grace of giving"* and rich generosity. He also encourages the Corinthians to *"excel"* in giving and to honor God in the process.

Paul also writes of coming to collect a *"pledge"* of support. Some people think of pledges as unscriptural or problematic. Paul's purpose, however, is to remind the Corinthian church, as well as encourage them, that their planned and promised gift was important to the work of the ministry.

The following are key principles from these chapters in 2 Corinthians:

1. **Sacrificial giving is desired—not just "discretionary income" giving.**

   "And now, brothers, we want you to know about the grace that God has given the Macedonian churches. Out of the most severe trial, their overflowing joy and their extreme poverty welled up in rich generosity. For I testify that they gave as much as they were able, and even beyond their ability. Entirely on their own, they urgently pleaded with us for the privilege of sharing in this service to the saints" (2 Corinthians 8:1-3, emphasis mine).

2. **Giving as grace from God—a special gift just as important as other areas that are desired.**
   "But just as you excel in everything—in faith, in speech, in knowledge, in complete earnestness and in your love for us—see that you also excel in this grace of giving" (2 Corinthians 8:7, emphasis mine).

3. **Give first; complete what you start; your willingness of heart is important.**
   "And here is my advice about what is best for you in this matter: Last year you were the first not only to give but also to have the desire to do so. Now finish the work, so that your eager willingness to do it may be matched by your completion of it, according to your means. For if the willingness is there, the gift is acceptable according to what one has, not according to what he does not have" (2 Corinthians 8:10–12, emphasis mine).

4. **Giving honors the Lord and is seen by all.**
   "What is more, he was chosen by the churches to accompany us as we carry the offering, which we administer in order to honor the Lord himself and to show our eagerness to help. We want to avoid any criticism of the way we administer this liberal gift. For

we are taking pains to do what is right, not only in the eyes of the Lord but also in the eyes of men" (2 Corinthians 8:19-21, emphasis mine).

5. **Pledges are important to complete the work; giving comes from the heart; the heart is what matters to God.**

"So I thought it necessary to urge the brothers to visit you in advance and finish the arrangements for the generous gift you had promised. Then it will be ready as a generous gift, not as one grudgingly given. Remember this: Whoever sows sparingly will also reap sparingly, and whoever sows generously will also reap generously. Each man should give what he has decided in his heart to give, not reluctantly or under compulsion, for God loves a cheerful giver" (2 Corinthians 9:5-7, emphasis mine),

6. **Generous giving pleases God, and He is praised as a result.**

"You will be made rich in every way so that you can be generous on every occasion, and through us your generosity will result in thanksgiving to God. This service that you perform is not only supplying the needs of God's people but is also overflowing in many expressions of thanks to God. Because of the service by which you have proved yourselves, men will praise God for the obedience that accompanies your confession of the gospel of Christ, and for your generosity in sharing with them and with everyone else" (2 Corinthians 9:11-13, emphasis mine).

In his book *Real Prosperity—Biblical Principles of Material Possessions*, Gene Getz states: *"The Corinthian model provides us with a dynamic principle. Christians who are generous will motivate other Christians to be generous. Many believers today have not been taught to give, or, if they have been taught, they are not yet responsive. They need to see other Christians enthusiastically using their material possessions to further the work of God's kingdom, They need to*

*observe joyful giving so that they might respond with the
same enthusiasm." (p.49)*

God's focus—the giver

While not many scripture verses address our organizations,
crisis management or annual fund goals, a great deal of scripture passages speak about the giver/steward. This is God's
emphasis—the heart and soul of the giver/steward. He provides instruction, encouragement and guidelines for the giver.

If God places great emphasis on the steward, we as Christian
development professionals, church stewardship pastors, and
organizations must place our efforts, attention and emphasis
on the giver as well. Then our programs and organizations
will produce God-honoring development relationships that
connect God's people to God's work.

CHAPTER THREE

Key Development Principles

Larry Johnston, president of McConkey/Johnston, Inc., has been a friend and a mentor to me for a number of years. His research, writings and applied theories are well known and respected in Christian development circles. He has graciously allowed me to share these principles he has developed and expand upon them for this book.

These principles are designed to show how solid development concepts are consistent with and grounded in biblical principles. The development officer involved in the ministry of development should be well versed in these concepts in order to be as effective as possible. I believe in this world of changing standards it is also important for the individual to have a solid understanding of the biblical foundations of development. This will serve her or him well when faced with decisions that are not black and white.

1. The benefit principle
The benefit in giving always goes to the giver (Philippians 4:17-20).

This builds upon the scriptural principles from the previous chapter. Paul tells the Philippians that he is not so concerned with their gift, but that it is credited to their account. This shows us that God is concerned with *how* we steward our resources. He will bless those who give. God knows who is generous and who gives of himself and his resources.

So while we believe our organizations benefit from gifts, ultimately it is the giver who benefits through God's blessings. The giver also benefits through the exchange of good feelings from knowing he or she is making a difference in people's lives.

This could be misinterpreted to eliminate the altruistic motivation of a donor to give for the sake of giving, not just to get God's blessing. There is a fine line here, based on point of view. From their perspective, donors have a number of motivations to consider. Donors give as a result of faith, for thankfulness or sometimes out of guilt or duty. As development professionals, we cannot be in the business of manipulating a donor's spiritual motivations.

Wesley K. Willmer again writes, *"Biblical stewardship assumes we look with accountability to God for the blessings of wealth."* (Christian Stewardship Courier) Those with wealth are accountable to God to give. From this giving lifestyle they receive the joy and blessings of knowing they are obeying God through being wise stewards.

But from the organization's viewpoint, we must recognize God's perspective. God looks upon givers and is concerned with the how and why they give, as I established in chapters one and two. If, as a Christian organization, our concerns are God's, then it follows that we will focus on the giver and their priorities and needs.

2.   The emotion principle
Giving is predominantly emotional (Luke 18:18-23; 2 Corinthians 9:7).

In the Luke passage Jesus responded from His heart when the blind man called out for mercy. Everyone else thought he was a bother and didn't want to help. But Jesus knew in His heart that this man had faith and needed his help, and so he responded.

Paul encouraged the Corinthians to decide in their hearts what to give. This is where decisions about giving of ourselves are made. Even when an individual responds to facts and figures, in the end the person will feel good about the tangible data and decide to give.

In working with inner-city rescue missions, I observe how prevalent emotional giving is. For example, after analyzing their budgets, policies and procedures and sending employees down to the mission to serve a meal, corporations will respond generously to the need. The reason is not so much that all the grant-making criteria has been met, but rather that the hearts of their employees were deeply moved when they saw firsthand the needs of homeless people when they handed them a tray of food.

In our world of accountability, analysis, annual reports and budgets, we must not forget that a gift from an individual, corporation or even a foundation is greatly influenced by the hearts of real people who are making the decision to give.

3.   The treasure principle
Where your treasure is, there your heart will be. Where your heart is, there your treasure will be (Matthew 6:19-21).

This principle is straightforward—treasure and heart are inseparable. When donors give, their hearts go with the gift. When a donor has a heartfelt belief in a cause or ministry, gifts follow.

This gives tremendous direction to the development efforts of a Christian ministry. Programs should be designed to involve the heart and the treasure of a donor. To focus strictly on factual needs ignores the connection between what a donor thinks and feels. *A development program should also seek to involve a donor along with a gift and not just accept their good intentions in monetary gifts.* Seeking prayer and/or volunteer time from donors is a natural extension of their giving.

The act of giving is the completion of the desire of one's heart to do something good and to make a difference.

4. The principle of fruitfulness
Fruitfulness always invites blessings and rewards (Matthew 25:14-30).

Development programs must be fruitful. They are not a window dressing to show good intentions. A program must invest time and talents to increase giving and givers. This is wise stewardship on the part of the organization that is funded by sacrificial gifts.

If a ministry has a mailing list, the list must be cultivated if the organization wishes to nurture the relationship with those donors. Allowing the relationships to dwindle away due to a lack of proper communication is not good stewardship. It costs much more to acquire new donors than to reactivate and involve lapsed donors.

Likewise, if a department has untrained but talented staff, an investment in training will bear fruit in the future. Development is constantly changing. New techniques are being tested and used. Donors are giving in different ways than in years past. Development must stay on the cutting edge. Training staff is wise stewardship in the use of resources.[1]

In this time of expanding needs and decreasing resources, a development program must balance the need to do more with the requirement to be fruitful in whatever is undertaken.

5. The principle of fruitlessness
Don't confuse activity with accomplishment. Fruitlessness invites disaster (John 15; Matthew 21).

---

[1] The Christian Leadership Alliance has developed a training program and professional certification called the Certified Stewardship Professional (CSP). You can learn more about it at www.Christian Leadership Alliance.com.

It is easy to become involved in a flurry of activities in our development efforts. Direct mail, newsletters, special events and grant proposals consume much time and effort. But are they producing the most effective return on investment? If development programs show more activity than results, they must be subject to careful scrutiny. What are the goals of the program? Are they net results or long-term cultivation? These questions must be asked before a program is launched.

For example, special events take a great deal of time and resources. Some organizations live by them. Others find the net results unacceptable. Or, some field representatives make plenty of calls on prospective donors. But what are the numbers and types of gifts received as a result of these calls? This must be carefully examined. Short-term results should not be asked to sacrifice long-term relationships. Effective and efficient programs should seek a balance between the present needs and the future.

In our age of accountability, we must be ready to show how our activities are bearing fruit. And then we must be willing to take the necessary steps to increase the effective programs and eliminate the ineffective ones.

6.   The principle of quantification
Development can and must be measured.

There are many ways to measure development efforts. Statistical analysis of direct mail programs, goal-setting for special events and monthly income reports for income-generating projects are all methods for measuring the status and effectiveness of programs.

What must be avoided is the tendency to start a program and not measure it. I have met with boards and executive directors in an effort to improve their development efforts. When I find there are no measuring processes in place, it is difficult to know where to begin. *"If you do not have a target, you hit the bull's-eye every time"* is a well-known maxim. It also follows that you can make the bull's-eye any size you want if you have no system for measurement. To create a well-run, effective and efficient development program, you must establish and maintain a system of measuring success.

7. The principle of dissipation
Development must direct its efforts at income-producing activities, or it will be burdened with busy-ness.

It is a natural evolution of growing development efforts to add programs such as public relations, community relations, volunteer relations and church relations. While these are important to the work of the ministry and should be a part of the development department, it is important to keep them in balance to income-producing programs.

Budgets for income-producing programs should be a higher priority than those for non-income producing programs. The return-on-investment (ROI) must always be considered as part of wise stewardship.

One organization I served with was in the process of building the development program. During that time the president decided to add five public relations employees to publicize upcoming concerts and tours. These were all under the development department budget. The experiment failed due to lack of planning and proper evaluation. And in the process the development budget and return on investment looked like a failure.

Time management is another area where key development personnel can lose focus. Public relations and other such activities can be time- consuming. It is important to keep a balance between those activities and time spent with key donors or planning direct mail programs.

Wise stewardship of resources includes staff, budget and time, all of which must be considered in the planning process. It is also showing sensitivity to the donors by using wise steward-ship in the development process. All donors want to be appre-ciated and cared for. But donors also recognizes that good development programs cost time and money. They want their gifts to be used as wisely as possible—and this includes staff management.

8. The principle of the critical few
Focus on what and who are really important. Twenty percent of the activities will produce eighty percent of the results (Luke 10).

It is often said that a few people always get all the work done when it comes to volunteering, whether it be in a church, a school or a special event. There are always those dedicated individuals who rise to the occasion and get the job done. This 80/20 rule is true in development as well. As will be shown in chapter four, the few givers from the top of a donor pyramid are the ones who give the most in total dollars to an organi-zation. These critical few are the people whose gifts carry the organization further faster.

Because the development department has little extra time and usually no extra budget, focusing efforts on these critical few donors is a wise use of time and resources. Strategies that allow the director of development and/or executive director to build relationships with these key people should receive pri-ority in the annual planning.

This is not to say that the other 80 percent of the donors are not important, nor should they be overlooked. The next peo-ple to move into the top 20 percent will likely come from there! Every relationship and gift are important to the organi-zation. But in setting goals and priorities, it is wise to consider the key relationships that will help the organization the most, and then plan accordingly.

Mennonite Church Canada
Resource Centre
600 Shaftesbury Blvd., Winnipeg, MB R3P 0M4
Toll-free: 1-866-888-6785

9. The principle of inspection
You get what you inspect, not what you expect.

This principle deals with the internal workings of a development office. The chief development officer or CEO must stay
in touch with her or his staff, goals and results of development
efforts. It is not effective nor is it profitable to start a project
and then ask to see the results six months later. Good development means good management and accountability. Stay in
touch with the internal as well as external relationships in the
development area. As my friend Larry Johnston once said to
me, *"get the numbers or the numbers will get you!"*

Much could be said regarding the development team. But that
would be another book. I will say only that the balance
between inspection, trust, staff members and leadership of the
team is delicate. Development is a demanding profession, and
creating a solid team takes a well-rounded effort combining
inspection and trust.

10. The principle of natural prospects
*Jerusalem, Judea, then Samaria. Start with those already com-
mitted, then expand (Acts 1:8).*

As Jesus sent out his disciples to build his kingdom, He gave
them some strategic marketing tips. First, start with
Jerusalem, where people know you and believe you. Second,
go out to Judea, where people have heard about you but need
more information. Finally, go out to the world, to areas that
have never heard of you and your message.

It seems logical to apply this to our efforts of adding supporters to our organizations. First, we should ask those who
already have shown they care about our organizations to support us again. This has proven to be a successful and cost-
effective strategy. It is much less expensive to ask a current
donor to give again than it is to go out and find a first-time
donor.

Second, go out the community. In some cases this is a geographical community, and in other cases it is the greater Christian community. People here may believe in your cause but need more information, or maybe have never been asked to give.

Finally, go out to the world (your world, of course). This might be a mail acquisition to your city, state or other countries. This region can be the most difficult to raise funds in, and the ROI may be low. Prospective donors are new to your organization and are essentially a cold call. It follows that this group is developed over the long haul and is not the first group you go to for immediate needs.

If a development staff follows these principles, its organization will be grounded on solid, effective and accountable guidelines. Not only will the staff be more effective, but with the accountability to donors, a more positive, lasting relationship will develop.

SECTION TWO

Stewardship As a Lifestyle

CHAPTER FOUR

Living a Lifestyle

A way of life is quite a notion. Most of us choose our way of life without reflection. Maybe when we look back over our lives we consider *how* we looked at life.

I think we all look at life through our own filters. Filters are built or clogged with the experiences, teaching, and learning that we go through. Of course, we are also God-designed, and our DNA is consistent throughout our lifetime. But I think when it comes to certain issues, feelings, or opinions, we determine how we will live our lives based on those filters.

The filter of knowledge, understanding, and experience in the area of the stewardship lifestyle is clogged in the church, the pastor, and the follower of Jesus. Our lifestyle filter is filled up with tradition, ritual, resentment, history, doctrine, denominational rules, and other types of parameters. This is not to say that this list is wrong or evil. It is just that as we go through life, one person may see a tradition as a positive in their life, and another may look at that same tradition and see it as a hindrance to their faith journey.

What is a lifestyle? I have heard it said we can live a rugged lifestyle, a faithful lifestyle, a dangerous lifestyle, and so on. But a lifestyle of stewardship? What does stewardship have to do with how we look at life or how we live our lives?

I wish to introduce a new definition of stewardship as lifestyle—a lifestyle that impacts all areas of our lives if we allow it. I hope to offer biblical and experiential evidence that challenges you to look at stewardship as a God-designed lifestyle, and therefore one of peace, joy, fulfillment, and provision. This lifestyle combines a life of faith with a life of compassion and action. It is a lifestyle of theology, philosophy, and hands-on experience.

What is the first thought that comes to mind if someone asks you the definition of stewardship? Do you relate to any of these people and their views?

The problem
One Sunday, after the pastor taught a message on stewardship during the service, a group of congregants stand in the church foyer. A Builder age member says, "I sure wish the pastor didn't have to beg for money all of the time. It seems that all our church is about is asking for money. In my day, we didn't have to ask so much."

A younger Baby Boomer agrees, "Yes, I think that is twice this year that Pastor taught on stewardship. I wonder how bad it is going to get. I give all I can, but there are other things that I think God can do with my money."

An even younger member responds, "I have a young family and I just do not have enough extra to give to the church right now."

A long-time member complains, "Why does the pastor have to keep asking for money? I have been going here for twenty years and we always meet our budget. Our baskets always seem to be full when they are gathered up."

A visitor to the church overhears the conversation and speaks up, "This is my first time here and I'm not sure if I will come back. The first thing I hear about is money and why the church needs it. I am not sure I can trust a new organization that quickly. It may take more time."

Another visitor interrupts, "Just what I thought, heavy on fundraising, light on biblical content. We will visit a new church next week."

"We have never been to a church before," says yet another visitor to their spouse as they get into their car—an unbeliever who overheard the people talking in the foyer . "But it sure seems like the members here complain about money."

These conversations prompt us to ask key questions including: Is money the problem? Or could it be that pastors and leaders have never learned how to teach stewardship correctly? Is stewardship about asking and budgets? Or is it about the stewards' walk with Christ and how they view their time on earth? Is it about ownership and idols? Or is it about bodies and buildings?

Church leaders feel comfortable communicating biblical truths from church pulpits, and they challenge, teach, inspire, and encourage their congregants. They remain very uncomfortable teaching about giving, stewardship, and money, however. These beliefs must be addressed in a straightforward manner with the bible as a guide. Leaders must not compromise on how to teach people to be good stewards.

There are many Builder, Boomer, Buster and Millennial-age pastors who believe that since the Builder generation started new churches, ministries, and non-profit organizations after World War II, teaching stewardship in the church has declined steadily. Pastors receive little training in seminaries and theological schools and the secular fundraising profession leads the way. As each new generation matures and begins volunteering and funding church and parachurch ministries, they have no teaching to guide them. The research shows little or no difference in motivation for giving between Christian or non-Christian donors.[2]

[1] George Barna, "Churches Lose Financial Ground in 2000," The Barna Report, June 5, 2001, www.barna.org, (accessed October 1, 2006).

Because pastors have little to no formal training in this area, they resort to their own personal strategies or the latest technique. They tend to be uncomfortable with the subject, yet know that it spiritually impacts everyone in their congregations.[3]

So the pastor reaches the foyer and begins discussions with the congregants. The pastor asks, "What did you think of my message? Was I too hard on the financial part?"

The various congregants respond less than honestly, "No pastor, you were right on. That is the message that our church needs to hear. I just hope they were all listening." Ironically, the pastor leaves that day believing the offering next week will meet his budget needs.

This simplistic story illustrates one of the problems of inadequate understanding of the true meaning of stewardship. Churches face inadequate teaching, wrong attitudes, and a lack of generosity in the church of Jesus Christ, which negatively impacts the organizations and the journey of stewards as they follow God.

Stewardship as a Lifestyle
A Christian's life is measured by many things. Scripture articulates some agreed-upon priorities: love, faith, fruit of the spirit, honesty, turning the other cheek, taking care of widows and orphans, prayer, keeping the commandments, and sharing the gospel. Bruce Wilkinson suggests there is another judgment, a time where Jesus Christ will ask each believer in Jesus what they have done with what He entrusted to them.[4] Paul refers to this judgment when he writes, "not that I am looking for a gift, but I am looking for what may be credited to your account" (Phil. 4:17 NIV). This suggests that each Christian has an eternal measurement of his or her stewardship here on earth and will be held accountable.

---

[3] Gene A. Getz, *A Biblical Theology of Material Possessions* (Chicago: Moody Press, 1990), 11.
[4] Bruce Wilkinson, *A Life God Rewards: Why Everything You Do Today Matters Forever* (Sisters, OR: Multnomah, 2002), 47.

Many critics write about contemporary lifestyles. There is a clear distinction between North American lifestyles and lifestyles in impoverished countries.[5] The world continues to evolve into have and have-not societies despite efforts to prevent this from happening.[6] It has been said one can tell someone's priorities by looking at their checkbook. Jacques Ellul states, *"Money has come to represent a certain type of 'spiritual' power in the contemporary society."*[7] This spiritual power controls how individuals think about, spend, save, loan, or give money. It is deep within each person and can be healthy or destructive. This power cannot easily be controlled, and some stewardship writers have determined the only way not to be controlled by money is to give it away.[8]

It is important to think of stewardship as a comprehensive approach to life, and explore how often Jesus spoke of money and its hold on human life. God is concerned with what individuals do with their money. It is a major power in a person's life, and it can produce much good through wise earning, investment, saving, and giving. In contrast, it can produce idolatry, accumulation, greed, jealousy, divorce, and rejection of God as the owner of all creation. Through giving, this dangerous power can be held in check. Ellul writes, *"The law of money is the law of accumulation, of buying and selling. That is why the only way to overcome the 'spiritual' power of money, is to give our money away, thus desacralizing it and freeing us from its control."*[9]

A lifestyle of stewardship is more than a strategy. A strategy focuses on a teachable method for the church and other

[5] Robert Richards, "The Economics Underlying Stewardship: Creation and Distribution of Wealth," Luther Seminary Stewardship Resource Database, http://www.luthersem.edu/ stewardship/resource_detail.asp?resource_id=974 (accessed November 28, 2007).
[6] Ibid.
[7] Jacques Ellul, *Violence: Reflections from a Christian Perspective*, trans. Cecilia Gaul Kings (New York: Seabury, 1969), under "The Fight of Faith," http://www.religion-online.org/showchapter.asp?title=573&C=715 (accessed December 3, 2007).
[8] Ibid.
[9] Ibid.

donors to communicate the raising of funds as a lifestyle. A lifestyle, however, reflects the steward's relationship with God. The relationship between Creator and creation is holy and defined by actions. A stewardship lifestyle, therefore, reflects an individual's relationship with God and the desired choices the individual makes as a result of that relationship.

Lifestyle Principle #1
We are encouraged to excel in the grace of giving,
and seek to be generous on every occasion. The goal
is to be known for our generosity.

CHAPTER FIVE

A New Stewardship:
Relationship with the Owner

Wikipedia defines Stewardship as personal responsibility for taking care of another person's property or financial affairs or in religious orders taking care of finances.[10] To be a steward requires a relationship with the owner. To be a steward is to serve the master as the servants who were rewarded did in the parable of the talents.[11] The servants received the master's pleasure through their wise stewardship of the ten talents and again the five talents.

Why would a steward want to please the owner? Because they are in relationship. There must be a relationship for the Owner-Steward to be successful. Some might think this is a boss-slave relationship. Our relationship with the Creator God is far from this. We have a relationship that is loving and generous. It is a relationship where the Owner is ready to give at every opportunity, and the Owner's desire is for us to enjoy, use, and multiply the gifts the Owner gives us. It is also the Owner's desire that we, in turn, become loving and generous in all areas of our lives.

So we see that in order to understand and live stewardship as a lifestyle, we must first have a relationship with the Owner, our God. One must be in relationship with the God of the

10 Wikipedia, accessed 5-20-09
11 Matthew 25:14-30

Universe, the Creator of all in order to be a steward. This is the same as the original stewards of the garden—Adam and Eve. Their lives were to be spent tending to the wonderful garden and living in relationship with God. When they disobeyed God it was not because of poor gardening, it was because the relationship was broken.

So it is with each of us. In order to be a steward of the wonderful garden we call life, we must have a relationship with the Owner. It is through this relationship that we seek to grow in our lifestyle of stewardship.

Lifestyle Principle #2
Stewardship is a lifestyle based on an understanding that everything comes from God. This understanding results in living a generous lifestyle integrated with our faith in Jesus Christ.

CHAPTER SIX

The Journey of the Steward

You have heard the saying, *"we are born with nothing, and we die with nothing."* Taken by itself it can be a discouraging saying. But when you look at this in light of stewardship, it clarifies everything!

For believers in Jesus Christ, each day is a journey with God, and stewardship becomes a daily aspect of our decision-making as well as setting priorities.

Stewardship decisions include how much time to spend in prayer and study God's Word, how much time to spend with spouses or children, how many of our talents to share with a charity or a ministry, and how much to keep for one's self.

Principle #3
God is more concerned with the journey of the steward, than with our budgets and goals.

The Stewardship Investment Process

On behalf of the Owner the Steward, wisely invests time, talent, resources, priorities, environment and relationships. The Steward knows this is a relationship of accountability. → The Local Church / The Church Institution / Parachurch Ministry → The Mission / The Front Lines of Ministry / The Work of the Gospel / The Cause

Figure 2

What is it about our journey that interests God? The answer goes back to our understanding of stewardship. God is concerned with abiding with us every day. Our walk in the Spirit is God's true desire for us. To want the things of God in our everyday lives is our goal as followers of Jesus. So it follows if we walk with God and abide with God, we will seek to think and do the things that Jesus would. We demonstrate this through our decisions, priorities, words, and deeds. We would try to please the Father (Owner) just as Jesus (Son/Steward) did during his time on earth.

In our ministries we are too self-centered. We have come to believe we as an organization are God's chosen and the organization's goals must be above all else. This is in conflict with God's concern with people, relationships, and their interaction with their Creator.

Organizations are not the enemy, just as money is not evil (the love of money is evil). But the prioritizing of the organization's goals and budgets above the relationship with the steward is when the line gets crossed and we cease following God's plan. Trouble follows.

Mennonite Church Canada
Resource Centre
600 Shaftesbury Blvd., Winnipeg, MB R3P 0M4
Toll-free: 1-866-888-6785

CHAPTER SEVEN

Stewardship as Transformation

The *Encarta World English Dictionary* defines transformation as *"a complete change, usually into something with an improved appearance or usefulness [and] the act or process of transforming somebody or something."*[12] This definition relates to the process of viewing stewardship as transformation. As individuals are transformed into God's image they take on God's view of creation and of their use of resources.

Transformation is a lifelong process. Scott Rodin writes in *Revolution in Generosity*:

The Christian life is a journey of transformation. From conversion to final glory we are called into a process of constant change, breaking away from the bondage of our old sinful nature and embracing the freedom of God's transforming grace. Our vocation involves dying to self and living for Christ. It requires us to lose a counterfeit life in order to find our true life. It is a shedding of our old nature and putting on Christ. It is a quest that promises nothing less than our re-creation as a new, holy and Christ-like child of God. While we will never attain the full end of this quest on this side of heaven, we are nonetheless compelled by the grace of God to enter unequivocally and sacrificially into the pursuit.[13]

---

[12] *Encarta World English Dictionary*, 1999, "transformation."
[13] R. Scott Rodin, *Revolution in Generosity* (Chicago: Moody Press, 2008).

Transformation is central to the future of stewardship education, and demands examination of the theological foundations
of a relationship with Christ. Key questions include: What is
the relationship that stewards have with God? How do stewards regard the possessions and resources God entrusted to
them? How do these views and values influence stewards so
they live differently and are transformed?

These questions have complicated answers. First, there is the
spiritual response to transformation. Within each Christian is
the power to be transformed by the Holy Spirit, and a Christian's life in following Christ brings a new spiritual understanding. For example, the book of Hebrews asserts that
individuals should desire deeper spiritual things rather than to
feed on milk, implying that they are still spiritual children
(Heb. 5:12-14). To be transformed is to hold the identity of
the steward deep within the soul, and to see eternal things the
way God does. In *The Treasure Principle* Randy Alcorn
describes the eternal perspective as one of his six principles:
seek the arrow, not the dot.[14] This implies that Christians
should focus on the journey, on the process of becoming more
like Christ, more loving, more faithful, and more generous.

A second aspect of transformation is its reality for our life on
earth. In this perspective, giving is comprehensive and
includes money, time, a caring spirit, relationships, and every
opportunity to be generous.

Transformation is a lifelong process, and transformational
stewardship is of value in a stewards' journey. God is more
concerned with a stewards' journey than with the budgets and
goals of churches and ministries. To act as transformed stewards requires a change in attitude and action. These transformed attitudes are demonstrated in the heart of stewards
and how they respond to those in need. Transformed spirits

[14] Randy Alcorn, *The Treasure Principle: Discovering the Secret of Joyful
Giving* (Sisters, OR: Multnomah Press, 2001), 49.

are sensitive to opportunities to be generous, rather than to accumulate, and actions follow transformed attitudes. Transformed stewards are generous, looking to be examples of giving. They also encourage others to be generous. They will seek to be noticed only when it encourages others to give rather than for the sake of personal acclaim.

Principle #4
We must move from transactional giving to transformational stewardship.

Many in the stewardship profession are concerned with the movement to transactional giving among nonprofits, churches, and parachurch ministries. Giving to the local church has become a transaction that purchases something, such as a balanced budget, building renovations, or a mission trip. This type of teaching and modeling results in the loss of spiritual significance to giving and generosity. Giving as a purchase or transaction renders the act of giving self-serving and of little spiritual value. The act of generosity without spiritual significance leads to a desire to acquire things, emphasizing the value of earthly things.

This desire conflicts with scripture. For example, Psalm 24:1 asserts, *"The earth is the Lord's and everything in it and all who dwell in it,"* and Paul writes, *"Just as you excel in everything, in love, in faith, and in your earnestness for us, see also that you excel in this grace of giving"* (2 Cor. 8:7). Followers of Jesus (stewards) can seek to be excellent in giving and be known as people of love, faith, and generosity.

A third aspect of stewardship as transformation is the resulting change of focus. For many in the twenty-first century, human life is filled with goals and the desire to achieve: a successful career, a good marriage, material possessions. In Western culture, when individuals achieve a certain stage in life, they expect their income to grow, and income growth enables individuals to purchase more and accumulate possessions. Christine Roush in her book, *Swimming Upstream* writes,

"Transformed stewards, however, focus on eternal things. Jesus directs his followers to seek the things of the Kingdom, and many scriptures challenge Christians to trust in heavenly things. Transformed stewards enjoy the things of this world that the Lord has allowed them to use during their lifetimes, but they do not value them in the same way they value eternal things of God that will last for eternity."[15]

The final point of a transformed steward is a change of heart. Transformed stewards give from an internal motivation deep within the spirit. Transformed stewards are transformed by the renewing of their minds through their relationships with God in Jesus Christ. Their sense of God's direction in how to give their time, talent, and treasure motivates their generosity, rather than coercion by the latest marketing gimmick or transactional offering challenge. Each time transformed stewards consider an opportunity to be generous, they gain another chance to communicate with the Creator, ask for wisdom and seek to be good stewards. This discernment and response is rewarded with God's peace, wisdom and multiplied impact (Luke 6:38).

Stewardship as a Lifestyle: Future Impact on the Church and Parachurch

The impact of transformational giving on the future church could be immense. Pastors could teach stewardship as part of the Christian life without guilt, shame, or fear. Church members could be generous as a way of life rather than only during fund raising campaigns. Young, emerging congregations could teach that a stewardship filter views the entirety of life as an opportunity to be a great steward.

The overall impact of teaching and learning about stewardship as a lifestyle would have a positive effect on seminaries, pastors, parachurch ministries, and followers of Jesus

---

[15] Christine Roush, *Swimming Upstream*, Kohler, WI: Design Group International, 2009.

Christ.[16] The newly created momentum could be a catalyst for the next generation of evangelism and leadership development as they equip and grow the body of Christ.

Principle #5
We in the local church and ministry organizations should put our emphasis where God puts his emphasis: the relationship with the steward.

---

[16] For more background on the idea of comprehensive stewardship education across congregations and church-related institutions, see: Mark L. Vincent, *A Stewardship Manifest*, Kohler, WI, Design Group International, 2000. It is a downloadable document available for all e-readers at www.DesignGroupInternational.com.

SECTION THREE

Implementing
the Ministry of
Development Philosophy

CHAPTER EIGHT

Development Concepts

After establishing the role of development as part of God's plan for his followers and highlighting the corresponding principles, we can apply them to current development programs and strategies.

There are basic philosophies and practices accepted by non-profit organizations. If development is to be ministry, it must not only follow scriptural standards, but it must also function at a level of quality consistent with common development philosophies and practices of the day.

The following development concepts are widely accepted as standards of applying development theory. Understanding these applications forms a basis for applying the ministry of development examples to be covered later.

Donor pyramid
A foundational principle is the donor pyramid. It is a graphic representation of the statistical analysis of the number of donors and how much they give to an organization within a specific period of time. In Figure 3 we see there are more donors (corresponding to the larger size of the base of the pyramid) at the lower level of giving. This may seem like common sense, as many organizations are built by the gifts of grassroots donors.

Some organizations, such as rescue missions, crisis pregnancy centers and camps, have historically relied on the bottom portion of the pyramid. They have many donors who give smaller amounts. This can be due to the type of donor who gives to the organization, the method used to ask them for support, or a combination of both.

The middle section of the pyramid represents the donors who give more than the bottom segment during a specific period of time. The narrowing of the pyramid means there are fewer donors in this group.

These donors may have given more than one time in a year, or have given larger individual gifts. Often these are donors who respond to a monthly partner program, enabling them to give a larger cumulative amount through frequent smaller gifts. Also in this group are smaller grants from family foundations, businesses and service organizations.

At the top of the pyramid are those critical few who give larger gifts to the organization. While these donors give larger gifts, there are fewer of them in most organizations. These donors usually give once or twice a year. This is not always true, but these donors often plan major gifts, perhaps coinciding with quarterly dividend payments, or year-end tax and giving planning. Corporate and foundation grants are often included in this portion of the pyramid.

This basic donor pyramid analysis is consistent for most nonprofit organizations, whether they be ministries, schools, hospitals or churches.

The donor pyramid demonstrates that people give at a variety of levels. It destroys the myth that if we ask everyone the same way for the same amount we will reach our goal. This never happens because people give at various levels based on their treasure, not our needs. Deuteronomy 16:17 bears repeating: *"Each of you must bring a gift in proportion to the way the*

Capital Giving

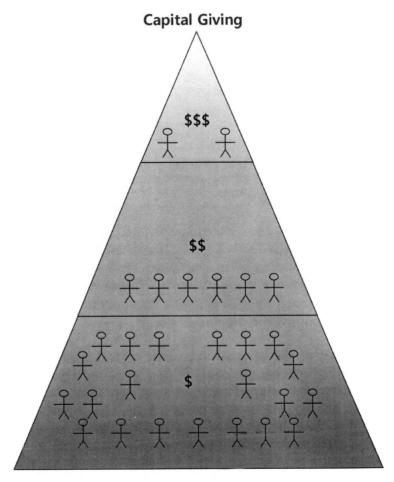

Figure 3

Lord your God has blessed you." We have all been blessed differently and therefore give differently.

The donor pyramid is consistent with scripture and is proven within the realities of nonprofit giving. Each ministry should begin analyzing its donor pyramid to better understand its donors' giving patterns and therefore their relationship with the ministry.

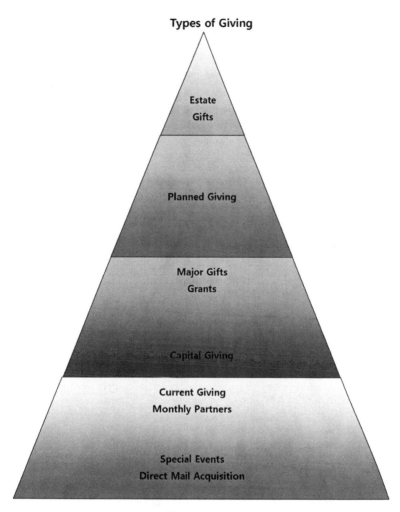

Figure 4

Current giving

Current giving is raising funds designated to the annual operations of an organization. Sometimes referred to as the annual fund, these gifts are raised every year within the defined fiscal calendar. Throughout the year, a variety of programs and projects asks donors to give to the ministry to enable it to accomplish its mission through its current facilities and programs. Current giving is generally for programs in the current year.

John R. Frank

The motivations for current giving donors are as diverse as the cause of the organization. Current giving donors are needed to make a difference in the present of the organization. Therefore, they become an integral part of the current programs and ministries. Their involvement can be through time, talent and treasure, and each should be valued and appreciated by the ministry.

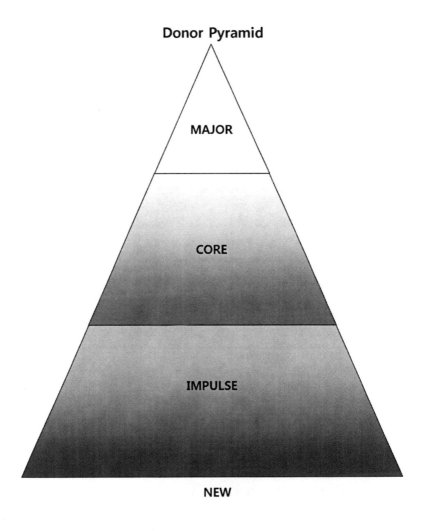

Figure 5

Current giving donors are the lifeblood of every ministry. They believe in the cause of the organization and reaffirm their commitment every time they give. They come from varied backgrounds, with mixed demographics, psycho-graphics and geographics. But knowing their giving patterns and how to connect them to the ministry is critical to the success of the development program.

Impulse donors may give once or twice a year, or many times at very small amounts. These donors usually give to the following types of programs or projects:

> Direct mail
> Acquisition (direct mail, radio, television)
> Special events

Core donors give at a higher level through either larger gifts or more frequent giving. They generally respond to the following:

> Direct mail
> Monthly partner/membership programs
> Special events
> Proposals to small corporations
> Proposals to foundations/family foundations

Major donors give at a higher level and usually less often. They generally give at higher single-gift levels as well. A key donor also can be a medium-gift donor who gives regularly, such as a monthly donation of $200.

Successful development programs that reach this segment usually include the following:

> Personal major gift solicitation
> Proposals to corporations
> Proposals to foundations
> Highly specialized special events (such as high ticket auction)

The key to current giving programs is to understand that each level of giving has its own motivations and aspects of relationship building. People who live and give at the major donor level, for example, must be approached in a different manner than those who give and live at the impulse donor level. This is not to say you treat people based solely on their financial worth, but an effective current giving strategy will use programs and projects that build relationships with donors at all levels of the donor pyramid.

Capital giving
A capital campaign is a planned effort to raise a specific amount of funds for a specific project within a specific period of time.

This definition is the key to what separates capital giving from current giving. These funds are for specific projects, whereas amounts of capital funding are needed beyond the annual budgeted goals. Some budgets do have line items for capital needs on an annual basis, but those become part of the current giving strategy.

Capital projects could be a new building, remodeling, a new piece of equipment or a combination of all of these.

An arrow flowing from the top of the donor pyramid to the bottom would represent the strategy used in most successful capital campaigns. One of the key concepts that separates capital giving strategy from current giving strategy is this *sequential solicitation strategy*. This is where donors capable of the largest gifts are asked first to give. When these contacts have been made and gifts secured, the campaign moves to the next segment, and so on. This is usually the time to take the campaign public and exceed the goal with gifts and pledges.

This sequential solicitation strategy determines the success or failure of a campaign in most cases. While this top-to-bottom strategy can be and is often used within a current giving strategy, it is almost always used in successful campaigns because it takes the campaign further towards the goal more quickly and efficiently, and allows the campaign to adjust its final goal in light of what its largest donors are willing to contribute.

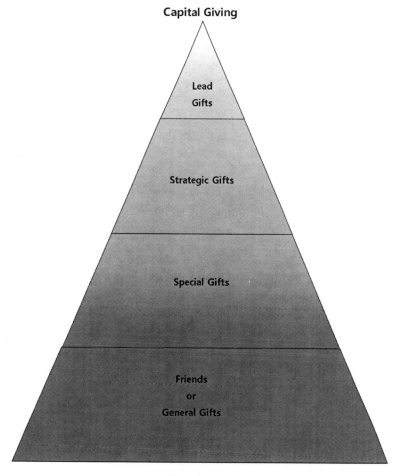

Capital Giving

Lead
Gifts

Strategic Gifts

Special Gifts

Friends
or
General Gifts

Figure 6

A capital campaign can be an opportunity to raise an organization to a new level of effectiveness. This happens not only in the development area but in the entire organization . The campaign encompasses the mission, vision and goals of the entire ministry. New volunteers and leaders are identified. New ideas for effectively pursuing mission come to light. Capital campaigns cannot be successful if it is looked upon as just another development project.

One organization I consulted for wanted to begin a capital campaign for a new building. When asked why they wanted to start, the answers of the development team and top management varied from, "We need it badly" to "Someone wants to buy our current, run-down building and make it into a parking lot." This did not demonstrate a clear vision for ministry in which a new facility would play a key role. But through the process of creating a campaign strategy, a vision for ministry, development goals, board development and staff training was developed. The organization was revitalized as it completed a successful campaign. And the campaign was the catalyst to rethink and retool many other aspects of the organization, such as overall development strategy, future board development, and staffing.

Campaigns can be exciting and challenging opportunities to reshape and transform an organization as well as efforts in development. But campaigns must also be successful. Donors are hesitant to invest in a poorly designed or managed campaign. Proper strategy and donor relations are key to the successful campaign that will launch a ministry to a new level of effectiveness and efficiency.

Key Development Principle: *People give to the future, not the past. The past only earns you the right to ask again.*

Planned giving
A planned gift requires careful consideration of your donors, their current and future needs, and their desire to give. This careful consideration results in gifts that demonstrate their caring and commitment to an organization. Planned giving is usually more complex than a current gift and usually involves professional estate planner or advisors.

Simply put, a planned gift needs planning to achieve the goals of the donor. This may involve the creation of a simple will that ensures a portion or all of an estate is sent to the desired organization. Planned giving may also involve more complex instruments such as charitable remainder trusts, annuities, pooled income funds or other tools. The broader definition of a planned gift could include a gift of stock or property given for operational concerns or for a capital campaign. This kind of giving takes significant planning to achieve the desired results for the donor and the organization.

Planned giving is an opportunity to minister to donors because of the types of giving it encompasses. While everyone should have a will, most Americans do not. Also, the current older generation has accumulated considerable wealth and is preparing to pass that along to the next generation. How do they know what to do? Whom can they trust? These situations present great opportunities for ministering to donors through education and counsel in planned giving. As professional development officers representing our organizations and ministries, we can assist people in leaving a legacy that they desire and may not have been able to do during their lifetimes.

An executive director of an inner-city rescue mission in the Midwest shared a story with me about an elderly woman he knew. She had supported the mission with small gifts for many years. The director was called upon a number of times to take the woman to the store, occasionally repair something or bring her to a mission event. He did this as an outreach to someone he believed was lonely and needed friendship. He did not try to sell her anything or ask her for a gift. He was surprised to receive a major gift from her estate after she passed away.

What this director did is not the only nor the best way to cultivate planned gifts. Meeting her felt needs was an effective strategy for receiving a planned gift, but there is a different point to the story. The woman was lonely and wanted to sense that she belonged to something and was cared for. The director showed he cared and was genuinely interested in her well-being. He did not manipulate or coerce her in any way. In turn, her gift was a demonstration of her appreciation for the relationship with the director and the mission.

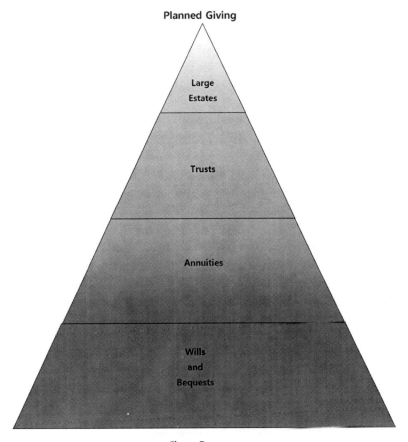

Figure 7

The challenge and sometime danger for every development professional involved in planned giving is to be sincere in building an honest relationship with each donor, yet in a way that can effectively generate planned gifts. This demands a delicate balance. If the development professional is motivated by a ministry of development philosophy, she or he will have clear direction when faced with ethical decisions.

The planned giving donor pyramid (Figure 6) shows that while there are estate gifts of all sizes, a well-established planned giving program provides consistent and frequent large gifts to ministries. Planned giving prepares an organization for the future. It is long-term in its design but can present opportunity for current gifts also.

Donor Motivation

It is important to note at this point how donors consider giving to each of the three different types of giving opportunities. Donor motivations are different for each type and must be considered as strategies are created and implemented.

Current Giving – Donors are motivated to give a current gift understanding the organization will use this gift for immediate needs such as staff, overhead, programs, etc. They know you will have to ask again as they give smaller gifts based on the need and your ask.

Capital Giving – A capital gift is usually made to a building project. They tend to give larger amounts over a three-year pledge payment period. This is because a building lasts many years. So they are motivated that their gift "keeps on giving" as long as the building is being used.

Planned/Estate Giving – A planned gift or a gift from an estate usually signifies a donor's values. They want to leave a legacy of their beliefs and causes they supported. The want to know their ultimate gift will be used for the cause they gave to during their lives of earning and generosity.

It is important to note that each motivation works with varying strategies. You cannot mix or match strategies and expect the same results. A campaign motivated donor often gives a higher amount than for an annual or current need. Most organizations cannot expect a donor to give the same amount for annual programs as they do for long-term gifts to a building project. It is a different motivation in the heart and mind of the donor. We development officers must respect this as we invite donors to give.

Win — Keep — Lift
The strategy of Win—Keep—Lift is a simple yet important concept for beginning and mature development departments to understand and implement. It forms a basic theory and strategy for starting and growing a development effort. (Figure 7)

Win
Win new donors for the ministry.

Every organization must add new friends and donors to stay strong and financially stable. *The involvement of more people in the ministry provides more opportunities for people to partner with and be connected to the work.* More students, more missions outreach and more beds for the homeless are some results of winning new friends.

Standard techniques for winning new friends include
    Direct mail acquisition
    Radio acquisition
    TV acquisition
    Tours
    Speakers bureau
    Special events
    Newsletter referrals
    Name solicitation
    Email
    Website
    eNewsletter
    Friends and family introduced by current donors

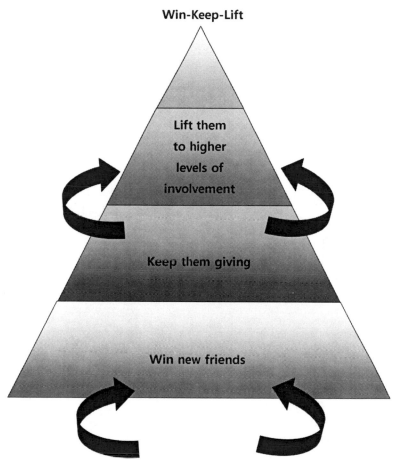

Figure 8

Keep
Keep current donors giving to the organization.

The goal of a development program is to create and enhance relationships with donors in such a way that they are encouraged to give again. Analysis of development programs proves that it is more cost effective to get a second or third gift from a donor than it is to labor to gain a first-time donor.

This concept is a good indicator of how successful an organization is at implementing the ministry of development. To which appeals do donors respond? How do donors feel about the programs and their effectiveness? Do the development programs and projects make it easier or more difficult for a donor to give a second time? How can we get to know our donors better?

There are many ways to minister to and draw closer to donors. They are examined more closely in the next chapter. Keeping donors involved and giving to an organization is critical to a successful development program. A program cannot be sustained by constantly working in an acquisition or "winning new donors" mode.

By creating and implementing a strategy to keep donors happy, involved and committed, a program will grow and not only successfully support the ministry, but will also minister to donors.

The following are some of the more successful methods that keep donors involved:
   Direct mail—regular monthly appeals
   Email
   eNewsletters
   Monthly partner program
   Special events—special invitation lists
   Personal contact—two or three times annually or as a
   follow-up to the first major gift
   Invitations/notices of all planned giving/estate planning seminars

Lift
Lift the donors to a higher level of commitment, involvement and giving.

The concept of life is what separates the beginning development program from the mature and successful one. Lifting a donor to a higher level of involvement and commitment to the organization generally means higher giving.

Everyone would like their donors to give more. But how is it done? How is an increased need communicated in such a way as to motivate donors to increase their giving?

Lifting donors to higher giving levels involves learning more about them, listening, responding through appropriate appeals and communication and thanking them accordingly.

Donors who increase their giving do so for a variety of reasons. Most, if not all, want their increase to be noticed. Sometimes their first gifts are just to test the waters to see how their gift is used or how they are treated. Was their receipt mailed promptly? Was a thank-you note or letter enclosed? Who was it from—a clerk or the head of the organization?

Keep in mind that not every donor increases his or her giving. This is a fact of the donor pyramid and the principle of the critical few. It takes a great deal of research, analysis, hard work and sometimes God working in miraculous ways to find these fantastic few who increase their giving.

Some programs that enhance the lifting of donors are
> Direct mail—occasional to frequent donors
> Email – to donors with a strong email relationship
> Personal contact
> Special events—a pledge or partner challenge
> Specific proposal
> Special invitations to all planned giving/estate planning seminars

Each concept and principle described here is proven to build a successful development program. While each organization is unique and has unique relationships with its donors, it must not fall victim to the myth of *we do not have to do it that way because we are different*. This naiveté shows a lack of wisdom by not learning from what other development departments have accomplished.

The development department or officer who wishes to build a successful ministry of development must first establish an understanding of what quality development activity is. Follow these principles by building a base of quality and proven development programs upon which to expand.

Ministering to donors while ignoring proven development principles is shortsighted.
After the foundation for a quality development is established, or even while it is being established, the ministry inherent to development will take it to a higher level. The higher calling of Christian development work can be the difference in creating a standard fund-raising program or a program that ministers to and partners with the donors and friends who have committed to the ministry.

CHAPTER NINE

How to Minister to Your Donors
Development Ministry in Action

Establishing a development effort that ministers to donors and is more than just a fund-raising program takes a concerted effort. It is easy to say you care about your donors and want the best for them. You want them to like your cause as well as your methods. You want them to trust you, love you and feel informed.

But as in most situations with nonprofits, these goals are not reached except by well-planned efforts. A development program does not become a ministry to the donors just because a board believes the executive director will prefer it or because ministry to donors can be validated with scripture.

To be an effective ministry, a development program must be proactive in its approach to inform and build relationships with donors. It must care about the needs of the donors *first*. It must place a high priority in meeting the needs of the donor. It must seek, as first priority, to assist the donor in realizing his stewardship goals. And this must not be just a marketing technique to appear caring.

The following projects are just some of the ways a development effort ministers to donors.

Prayer
To ask for prayer on behalf of the ministry is common among ministry organizations. Prayer requests in newsletters relay ongoing and urgent needs. It is important to the donor/reader/friend of the organization to know what the needs are. And as Christians partnering in the ministry, we need to know how to pray.

The other side of the issue is praying for the donors and *their* needs. As a ministry, do we have compassion for our givers and realize that they have hurts, concerns and problems? Do we realize how many of our partners see us as a type of "spiritual leader" in their lives— someone they look up to?

We can show leadership in this area by praying for our donors. In inner-city missions we pray for our clients; in overseas missions we pray for people groups and missionaries. So it follows we should pray for our donors as they give and pray for our ministries.

Donor prayer requests
Asking for prayer requests on the back of response devices is an effective way to encourage donors to write to a ministry. Consider designing the form to make it easy for them to respond by leaving a space at the bottom or on the back, and ask them to share their needs and concerns.

An effective follow-up after the staff has prayed for the request is to send a post card to the donor that lets him know request was honored. This not only lets the donor know his concern was prayed for, but it connects the staff member to the donor as well. This can be an effective method of bringing non-development staff members closer to the heartbeat of development—namely, the donors.

When this program was implemented in one ministry I assisted , staff members began keeping in touch with donors who had family problems, poor health or other concerns. Our ministry to people thus went beyond the gifts, and both donors and staff members were blessed.

Prayer updates
A successful approach to prayer support is including answers to prayer in a publication or letter. Designate an area of the publication to notify friends how God has answered their prayers concerning the ministry. This will show how the readers' prayers and concerns make a difference in the organization.

A local rescue mission found this technique forged relationships between donors and the staff. When staff members began praying for donors' needs, they began to realize these people had hurts and heartaches and needed the mission to care about them too. Praying was their way of connecting with the cause of homelessness. When the staff prayed for them, the donors were thankful and sensed a deeper relationship with the organization, a relationship beyond financial gifts. The staff began to view donors as more than just a means to an end of increased ministry because they received more money. Employees became an integral part of the ministry to the donors.

An organization will find many great opportunities to minister to their friends, givers and partners that will be rewarding and fulfilling—not manipulative—through a prayer ministry.

Appeals
Our partners and friends want to give to the ministry. They want to be informed of the genuine needs and concerns of the ministry. Much has been written about the abuse and overuse of direct mail. But studies and focus groups still show that many people want to be kept aware of ministry needs through regular, appropriate letters.

Here is the key point. What is appropriate communication? Jerry Huntsinger, President of Huntsinger & Jeffers, Inc. and a recognized authority on direct mail, wrote in the March

1994 issue of *Fund Raising Management Magazine* on the future of direct mail, "You'll have fewer donors on your mailing list, but you'll know them better and give them better treatment." Sixteen years after this was written, it is more true than ever.

Appropriate communication and better treatment can be defined differently for each organization and donor segment. Here are some areas with which to begin:

Honest letters
Sending honest, straightforward, non-manipulative appeals is a blessing to true givers. They will feel connected to the ministry and a sense of accomplishment knowing their gifts make a difference. This assists them in their desire to be wise stewards. From my experience as a development officer, I believe the donors want to know the true needs of the ministry. And when the timing is right for them to give to a project or need to which they are drawn, they will respond.

Urgent! Urgent! Crisis! Crisis!
So many donors tire of the urgent-gram or crisis letter. They want to help and many times will respond to true needs, but many organizations overuse this as a technique, thereby showing no respect for the donor. Donors are terribly hurt if they find out the crisis was only in the eyes of the nervous CEO or director of development, or worse, if the crisis is manufactured or exaggerated in order to raise money.

In these days of long-term financial planning versus hand-to-mouth, short-term management, donors do not know if this is a true emergency need or simply a strategy to meet annual budget goals. If crisis direct mail pieces continue, over time there is great donor attrition. Their giving frequency drops, and they may begin giving to another organization that appears more honest and less crisis-driven.

However, a true crisis does occasionally arise in an organization. Once again, true, forthright and honest appeals are still successful— that is, if a relationship of trust and integrity has been established.

After the PTL scandal in the 1980s, there was great concern for donor attrition and mistrust. Ministries who had established honest, caring relationships with their donors did not see a negative impact on giving. In fact, some saw an increase as donors sensed they were giving to an organization that would not mislead them. The organizations that had not established an integrity-laden development ministry found donors skeptical and hesitant to trust them.

I said to my staff at that time, and I still believe, if the PTL crisis produces wiser givers, those organizations who are doing their proper job in development have nothing to fear from the negative publicity that comes from such scandals.

An organization that was involved in the PTL issue, as well as many other situations, is the Evangelical Council for Financial Accountability. They offer a set of standards for Christian ministries in fundraising and overall financial issues (see the Appendix for their mailing address). They offer materials to assist development efforts in reporting to donors.

One technique used to show sincerity and honesty through direct mail is printing the following (or something similar that expresses the mission of your organization) on the back of a reply device:

> *The (ministry name) is a member of the Evangelical Council for Financial Accountability (ECFA). Membership in ECFA is your assurance that an organization adheres to the highest standards of Christian stewardship and ethical financial practices.*
>
> *This organization is supported entirely by the compassionate gifts of friends and receives no government funding.*

> *In all our communications, we endeavor to present the*
> *needs of the homeless [in this case a mission] and hurting*
> *with accuracy and honesty. We do not intend to create any*
> *feelings of obligation. Friends are invited to participate in*
> *the work of the mission only as they feel led by God to do*
> *so. We believe that God will meet the needs of the poor*
> *through the gifts of those who respond in this way.*
>
> *If gifts are received above a specific need, they will be*
> *used for mission programs where the need is greatest.*

This is one way to communicate the organization's intent to
the donor. It is not the correct style or content for every ministry but can be adapted if appropriate.

Stewardship Education
Direct mail can also play an important role in stewardship
education. By demonstrating the biblical model for fund raising, a direct mail appeal brings a positive impact on the donor.
It can also be used as a training and modeling tool for stewardship principles by emphasizing giving to the local church
and living a lifestyle of stewardship. Direct mail is a powerful
communication tool and can be very effective in influencing
the reader.

Quality, consistent and honest direct mail that appeals to the
proper target segment will find success and will be a vital ministry link with the donor. It can be a source of strong support
to the ministry which uses it wisely.

Giving clubs and partner programs
A giving club or partner program is a development project
that allows donors to give on a consistent schedule, or at a
consistent level or amount. They make the choices and the
organization provides consistent reminders. This may be in
the form of monthly donors or annual major gifts.

At first glance giving clubs may seem like a marketing technique. But upon investigating a well designed Christian giving

club, you will find a program designed to meet givers' needs and bring them closer to a ministry they care about. Monthly letters that treat them as a special friend, special events for club members, and sometimes appropriate gifts or premiums, promote a sense of family and connectedness to the ministry.

Giving clubs are not only a growing trend in donor demographics, they are also common sense. No one wants to be treated as a number on a mailing list. A club that is appropriately designed for a donor group's interests and giving ability is a good way for donors to give and be involved in a unique and special way. In so doing you *minister to the member.*

One club I designed was taking over for a program that was declining. The 2,000 members were not faithful, and giving had declined from $100,000 to $40,000 in two years. After redesigning and renaming the club as the *99 & ONE Club*, my team launched the new program by inviting the same 2,000 members; 1,500 rejoined. By writing to them on a monthly basis and providing consistent updates of the ministry, we saw their giving reach $295,000 that first year. With 500 new members the next year they gave $447,000.

These partners say they responded because of a focus on how giving would be used (all gifts went to the feeding and sheltering), because the club name communicated vision (Luke 15:4-6), and because the mission provided consistent updates and pledge reminders.

Trends in donors reported by George Barna and Judith Nichols confirm that many donors desire a monthly reminder from the organization to which they have made a commitment. This allows them to be faithful while not having to use their own reminder system.

Newsletters

Timely, informative and accurate ministry articles are always a blessing to the donor. While they may not always read every article, ministry partners will rejoice at seeing articles about

ministry success and pray when the executive director men-
tions a vital need in his or her article.

Many mailing lists have a wide range of donors—from strong
evangelical Christians to secular humanists who responded to
a mailing or event. Newsletters are a great opportunity to
share the Gospel in a new and applicable way—and maybe
plant a seed where one had not been planted before. They can
be a key ministry tool if designed and written with these goals
in mind.

The quality and readability of a newsletter is a key ingredient
as well. With all the in-house technology available today there
is no excuse for a poor quality newsletter. A well-designed
cover with masthead and well-written articles will draw the
reader in. If it looks too simple, the newsletter might appear to
lack quality. If it appears too slick, it can put off readers if it
is not consistent with the image of the organization.

A newsletter can be the heartbeat of a ministry and a way to
keep friends of the organization involved. But it must be written from the viewpoint of the reader/donor, not from the
viewpoint of the staff person. Each article must answer the
question, "Does our donor want to know this?" This differs
from the usual internal viewpoint: "Do *we* want the donor to
know this?" A balance of important information is needed,
but the newsletter must produced with the reader's perspective
in mind.

A mission where I served as director of development had a
newsletter long before any direct mail program had begun.
After years of aggressive name acquisition and a new direct
mail program, the newsletter still brought in $600,000 to
$800,000 each year. Faithful donors who used the return
envelope included with the newsletter considered it their
favorite and most comfortable method of communication
with the mission. To this day these donors prefer the newsletter over any other type of communication. That it is used as a

ministry information piece and not as an appeal proves the fund-raising abilities of newsletters.

Social Media

What about Social Media? We are watching the explosion of possibilities for development professional offered via technology. Much can be written about Facebook, Twitter, MySpace, and other Social Media developing almost daily. With all the possibilities, however, we must give the most attention to strategies that bring people closer to each other, and to our ministries. Each generation will find new and creative ways to communicate. But the PRINCIPLES of relationships and ministry will remain the same.

Relationships remain the cornerstone of Social Media. The tools are an extension of real life. Conversations usually begin face to face, continue over electronic media, and then are strengthened when people are face to face once more. Many might think Social Media is merely trendy or not conducive to building community, but we as development officers must always look to the future and the next generation of donors in order to learn and adapt to new forms of relationships. Then it is our job to reach out and connect these relationships to God's work!

Volunteers

The involvement of volunteers can be viewed as anything from a wonderful ministry opportunity to a major hassle for staff. The perspective depends on how the program is designed, and of course, on what the purpose is for having volunteers.

As mentioned earlier, a development ministry creates opportunities to connect God's people to God's work, assisting them in the wise stewardship of their time, treasures and talents. Volunteering is a wonderful way to connect and allow them to use their talents and time in moving the ministry forward.

Designing a volunteer program that ministers to the volunteer as well achieves the goal is the key to success. I suggest four basic components to planning a solid volunteer program: assessment, recruitment, management and appreciation.

Assessment
Design a volunteer program with results in mind. Communication with other staff is critical. In which areas can you use volunteers? How many? For how long? Is the work seasonal?

What type of volunteers do you need? Retired seniors? Stay-at-home mothers and fathers? Word processor operators and clerical support? Drivers and meal deliverers?

After the assessment is complete, the organization will know how adding volunteers can increase effectiveness and efficiency. They will know if volunteers add to or save on expense.

Recruitment
When it is known what type of volunteers are needed, the recruiting process can begin. Using the organization's newsletter is a good place to begin if there is a well-defined application procedure. Sending the notice to the entire mailing list could bring a large but unfocused response.

Consider asking current volunteers (if you have any) to invite friends and peers to volunteer. People who love the ministry and know the inside culture are great recruiters. They will share their story of feeling a part of the ministry, and yet will be realistic about the work and the tremendous needs you strive to meet. Word-of-mouth recruiting is the most effective.

A volunteer newsletter can be another way of recruiting volunteers. Specially written to a target group, it can be mailed or left at churches or retirement centers (if seniors are a target segment) to invite prospective volunteers to apply.

Management

Here is a key area of ministry, but an area where many organizations fail. Treating a volunteer as unpaid staff is a good place to start as you plan. Create a written job description and provide appropriate office supplies and, if appropriate, a desk to insure the volunteer is appreciated and valued.

But even more important than space and supplies is what happens on the first day. How do you welcome and introduce volunteers? This will demonstrate if your organization values the time and talents of its volunteers. Show volunteers how their work will make a difference in the cause. Introduce them to other key staff. Make sure they know where important rooms and supplies are. Do not force them to wander around looking for their work. Also, make sure the staff knows when new volunteers arrive for their first day. Put out the welcome mat!

Training your volunteers is key to ongoing success. Prepare a manual with procedures and policy. It is not necessary to overburden them with paper, but an appropriate amount of information about the organization, the corporate culture and how their work fits in will assist them in performing their duties.

As time goes on, make sure you maintain consistent communication with the volunteers. Select a volunteer coordinator from your staff, if possible. If not, use a volunteer newsletter. Also, train and follow up on staff who oversee volunteers in their departments.

In one organization we had fifteen to twenty senior volunteers come in every month to put out the newsletter. They would fold, staple, sort and bag by zip code—all 70,000 of them. Occasionally I would stop by to thank them and listen to their stories. But most importantly, I would share with them what was in the newsletter this month and how important their work was to the development efforts and to the entire ministry. I tried to convey to that we could not do it without them.

The other side of volunteer management is handling a volunteer who is not successful. He or she might be in the wrong position or is simply not qualified to volunteer in your organization. An application process and a probation period can help prevent this.

When this uncomfortable situation occurs, however, it must be dealt with fairly, with compassion and immediately. Allowing the situation to continue helps no one and undermines the quality of your volunteer program. Keep in mind that you can minister to someone as you assist her or him in finding the right place for their volunteer efforts.

Appreciation
Sometimes considered frivolous by budget-conscious ministry staff, this area is critical to a well-designed volunteer program. Whether it is board members (who are volunteers too), office personnel or parents who assist in a classroom, all should be recognized and appreciated for their efforts. In a society where time has become *the* invaluable resource, those who give of their time should be thanked and appreciated.

A letter, an annual banquet and 5, 10 or 15 year service pin all develop a sense of belonging and appreciation. Again, any means that you choose to convey your appreciation must be appropriate for the organization, its mission and context.

One volunteer appreciation event planned and implemented by our Director of Volunteer Efforts involved a Mexican dinner complete with decorations, music, and special gifts for the volunteers. The director had been in Mexico as a missionary and brought a wonderful, authentic atmosphere to the event. The volunteers were thrilled and appreciated.

The use of a quality volunteer program in a society where there is distance between neighbors, and even within congregations, can be a refreshing opportunity to minister to supporters and friends, while building a sense of family and community.

Board of directors

How do we minister to the board of directors? First, realize they are volunteers and (hopefully) donors. We must not take their commitment and sharing of talents and gifts for granted. If we approach our board members as men and women who care deeply about the ministry and are willing to be held accountable for its success, we will view them in a new light.

Are there ways to connect them to the ministry other than through monthly or quarterly meetings? Try hosting the meetings at various sites. This would refresh the board members with new surroundings as well as make them aware of the ministry taking place in each facility.

Also, have key staff members share successes and failures—if you are courageous enough— at each board meeting. Again, this refreshes board members and reminds them of why they agreed to their leading and governing role.

Another technique to minister to the board is to ask them to pray for specific staff members or departments. Assign staff to each board member and then update them on projects and, if appropriate, personal prayer needs. This reinforces their connection to the front lines of ministry and encourages the staff too. Remember that board members tire of long meetings about budgets and procedures, especially when there is not a reminder of their first love—the ministry, the cause, the reason they are there in the first place.[17]

Media

Ministering to the media through development programs takes careful planning and attention to detail. Members of the media are, by nature and profession, skeptical of any type of manipulation.

---

[17] From my consulting experience with boards and from using the Drucker Board Self-Assessment Tool, I learned the most neglected area causing concern among board members was *"How do we know if the mission statement is being carried out."* This critical area is the most important responsibility of the board, yet is often overlooked.

You must begin by understanding that the media need stories every day in order to do their job. They want to print or report what is happening, and they will definitely have their bias.

The media welcome clear, consistent and quality public service announcements. Press releases have a format determined by the type of media they are sent to (print, radio, TV, etc.). By following the proper format, an organization shows respect for the media's profession and their need to serve various audiences.

Inviting media to key events in the life of an organization draws them closer to the cause and erases misunderstandings they may have of Christian organizations. If funds and personnel allow, a media relations person can develop one-to-one relationships with media staff.

The key is honesty and integrity. If members of the media feel an organization is using them for publicity or is not completely truthful, they will not cooperate the next time. The last thing an organization wants is to fight the media or develop an adversarial relationship. This usually becomes a no-win situation.

If the organization is well-respected in an area, such as human services, it can become an expert for the media to call when needed. To serve as an honest, dependable resource for issues is a great way to serve the media.

As Christian ministries we are called to let our light shine. A relationship with the media can allow us to do this if we have an attitude of serving and ministering to them, instead of just a desire for free publicity.

Gifts and premiums
Ministering to our donors through appreciation gifts and/or premiums is a controversial subject. Some development strategists believe nothing should be sent to donors and no

gifts should be recognized other than with a receipt. Others take the opposite view, arguing that an appreciation gift is appropriate if the gift is consistent with the ministry (i.e. president is author of a book) and is beneficial to the donor, and can foster additional ministry or encourage further support from the donor and the donor's network of relationships.

I believe gifts are viable development tools if the following is considered:

- Are they appropriate for the image of the organization? A gold eagle statue, for example, might not be appropriate for a donor to a homeless shelter.

- Does the organization know enough about its donors to create appreciation programs?

- What is being rewarded? A direct mail response, a campaign pledge, a year of support, or as a simple thank you?

- Does the gift reflect or enhance the mission of the organization (the president's new book, for example)?

A appreciation program can be an effective way to minister to donors and their networks of relationships. An educational book or insert can uplift the giver. One ministry that I know of has various outreaches (radio, Christian school, senior home, etc.) and the president sends an insert message from Proverbs with every receipt.

We must be consistent with the biblical basis of stewardship. We should not promote giving gifts to get something in return. However, if the item or gift is consistent with our mission and we have an opportunity to truly minister to the donor, appreciation gifts can be appropriate.

Guidelines for development
What does an organization stand for? What will it do and what won't it do? What are its development standards?

These are issues each organization must wrestle with in the coming years. Changes in our legal systems will warrant more accountability and demand more licensing and permits.

By creating guidelines for development, a Christian ministry can be proactive in this area. Adhering to standards for its development efforts and then making these guidelines available to its donors is another tangible way an organization can minister to them.

I adapted the following guidelines for the Union Gospel Mission of Seattle when I was on staff. This document was then approved by the board of directors. I organized these principles from various sources and from Whitney Kuniholm's booklet *The Ministry of Fund Raising*, published by Prison Fellowship Ministries. Mr. Kuniholm's principles are well-thought-out guidelines that he graciously allowed me to adapt for my work with the Mission and for this book. His booklet is noted in my bibliography.

1. One leader
This ministry belongs to the Lord, not to any individual.

2. His vision
The Lord has apparently chosen to place his mantle of approval on the mission. Nevertheless, God gives and sometimes takes away. If God ever closes the doors to this work, we will accept God's leading and yield the outcome to him. Until then, we will devote every ounce of energy to the task at hand.

3. Honesty
One of the ways we can discern the Lord's will regarding our work is through the support God sends (or doesn't send) from his people. Therefore, during lean times we will make our needs known to our friends, but we will never resort to disrespectful and dishonorable methods of fund-raising, even when the needs are serious.

4. Partnership with the church
We will ask people not to support the organization until their obligations to the local church have been met.

5. Accountability in Stewardship
We consider the contributions we receive to be sent from loving people who have sacrificed to make their gifts possible. Our obligation, therefore, is to spend that money conservatively and wisely in continuing the ministry. Every penny is stretched as far as possible to serve the needs of today's homeless.

6. Accountability in Timeliness
We will receipt all donations as soon as possible.

7. Proper business practices
When we make a purchase, we will pay the invoice within 30 days if possible. We do not intend to use the vendor's money.

8. Accountability in Ethics
We will not try to raise more money than we need.

9. Mailing list
We will never sell or rent our mailing list to those wishing to use the names of our supporters. We will maintain the highest security on our list of supporters and friends.

10. Accountability to our Community
We will conform to the standards established by the Evangelical Council for Financial Accountability, the Better Business Bureau, and even our local Chamber of Commerce.

11. Biblical approach
All of our fund-raising practices will be based on biblical foundations, which will reflect all development as a ministry.

12. Statement of faith
Nothing in our development strategies may contradict our statement of faith. We will include our statement of faith

where appropriate or, if not provided in written form, its intent will be clear to the reader/donor.

13. Adherence to purpose statement/mission statement
We will involve donors and raise funds to meet the genuine needs of the ministry's programs. We will not raise funds or ask donors to support programs that are outside of our purpose statement. If we receive a gift that does not meet this criteria, we will contact the donor, inform him of our inability to meet his designated request and allow him to decide how to use his gifts appropriately.

14. Full disclosure
We will practice complete financial disclosure and stand accountable to the Lord, ourselves and our supporters in determining the need and in raising and spending the Lord's money. This will include publishing an annual report with audited financial statements, sending audited financial statements to anyone who requests them and honoring any reasonable request to inspect our financial records and expense reports.

15. Truthfulness in communication
All representations of fact, description of financial condition or narrative of events must be current, complete and accurate. We will not mislead anyone through written or photographic materials.

16. Role of persuasion
We will actively pursue heartfelt, generous and cheerful giving to the great work we have been given in this ministry. We do understand that we are

Compelled to	Be passionate — the needs touch human lives
	Be persuasive — the message must be told and understood
	Be urgent — the needs are immediate
	Have integrity — we represent Jesus Christ

Constrained to   *Present giving as an act of obedience to*
Jesus Christ
Be involved in fund-raising that meets biblical guidelines
Be straightforward and sincere in our relationships and communication
Carefully appeal to reason and emotion in our communication

17. Donor expectations
Appeals and communication must not create unrealistic expectations of what a donor's gift will accomplish.

18. Donor intent/designations
All statements made in appeals and specific donor requests must be honored.

19. Reporting
The development staff will seek to make accurate and timely reports on all development programs to the executive director, board of trustees and to reasonable requests.

20. Percentage compensation
The ministry will not work with any person or project involved in paying a percentage of what is raised or any other contingency. This conflicts with our biblical standards of keeping in the mind the needs of the giver.

21. Commissions and gifts to insiders
Employees, officers, directors and other principals (and their families) cannot accept finders' fees, commissions or payments of any kind from any person or entity doing business with the organization.

22. Acknowledgment of gifts in kind
All property or gifts in kind will be described accurately without a statement of the gifts' market value (unless proscribed by law). This is the responsibility of the donor.

23. Percentage of overall fund-raising costs
The annual fund-raising percentage will be determined by the annual budgeting process and approved by the board of trustees. Percentage guidelines for fund-raising costs cannot be used as standards for comparison with other organizations due to may variables, such as
- length of donor cultivation
- cost of name acquisition
- different allocation methods for determining program, management and fund-raising costs

24. Acting in the interest of the donor
In dealing with potential planned or deferred gifts, every effort must be made to avoid accepting any gift that would put the welfare of the donor in any hardship or place the future of the donor in jeopardy.

25. Financial advice
When dealing with persons regarding major estate assets, the organization will seek to guide and advise donors prior to receiving a commitment so as to insure that the needs of the family have been considered. The organization will encourage donors to consult with other professional advisors, such as accountants and attorneys. We should not compute a donor's taxes. We will receipt them for the proper gift and allow them to work with their tax accountants for proper usage.

26. Matching grants
The ministry will encourage use of matching grants provided the donor makes this clear when giving the gift and when both the gift and matching gift are properly accounted for and designated.

27. Endorsements
Endorsements may be used in development programs provided written approval has been attained concerning quotes, photographs, etc.

28. Consultants
The ministry may use consultants as necessary, provided:
- *The ministry retains total control of content of any donor communication*
- *A set price has been agreed to prior to any effort beginning*

29. Donor files
All donor information is confidential and will be treated as such. As a general policy, we will not publish donor names unless warranted by a specific project and given board approval.

30. Government funds
In accordance with the statement of faith and statement of purpose, the organization will not receive government funding that restricts the ministry in any way.

These guidelines are not right for every ministry or organization. But by making the effort to create this type of document and then making it available to donors, the organization will take a proactive step toward a stronger relationship with friends of the ministry.

This honest approach provides a refreshing change for donors and they will truly feel ministered to and appreciated.

Estate planning seminars
Hosting educational seminars benefits donors by providing much-needed guidance. Many organizations hold estate planning seminars, but careful attention should be given to the purpose. No, it's not wrong to follow up leads in hopes of being named a beneficiary of a will or a trust agreement. But again, a ministry's first goal should be to serve the donor.

We live in a time when estate planning is critical in allowing the donor a choice in how giving desires can be accomplished. The number of people who die without wills is high even though planned giving professionals host frequent seminars about writing wills. Many of our donors trust us and look to us for guidance. How will we respond to their trust? With a slick marketing brochure, or a well-planned program centered on building relationships and sharing information? The latter must be our desire.

Many organizations feel they are too small to start a planned giving program or offer seminars. There are many ways to start and build a program. Contact local professionals or attend a seminar of another organization to get ideas. Then begin serving donors in the best way available. There are national foundations for small Christian ministries that allow them to use their planned giving expertise and to be a part of the foundation. One I know of is the National Christian Community Foundation (www.nationalchristian.com). They offer this service to various organizations. Other sources might be a local Christian college or a large national ministry. Many times they can be of assistance through their own foundation.

As donors sense that the program is designed to assist them in a critical time of their lives, they become lifelong supporters of the work and continue this support with a gift at the time of their death. The ministry will know it has assisted someone in reaching the donor's stewardship goals in addition to receiving their gifts.

Tours

Many times nonprofit groups think no one knows or cares about how we do our work. But in this age of accountability, opening our doors can benefit the donor and the organization's image.

Hosting tours of your organizational headquarters or ministry sites is an excellent way of linking donors to your work. By inviting current donors or local pastors or even local businesses to see firsthand what is taking place behind the doors of the organization, these groups can be connected in ways never before achieved.

Design a tour program and then market it to appropriate churches, Sunday schools, businesses, school groups and donor groups. This will give people a firsthand connection with the organization. They will feel closer and be better informed. And even more, they become advocates for the cause.

CHAPTER TEN

Putting It All Together
Making Your Development Effort
a Ministry

Development professionals who desire to establish a development effort that ministers to donors must start with themselves. We are teachers and trainers in our staff leadership roles, so we must begin with ourselves.

Consider the following as starting points:

- Develop a personal study in biblical foundations for giving, stewardship and development.
- Examine your personal giving. Development officers *must* be givers to the organizations they serve, and not stop there.
- Network with other development professionals in Christian and non-religious organizations. Discuss methods and philosophies. Discover other ways of communicating principles of development ministry.
- Pray for your organization's donors. Thank God for them. Become their advocate in the organization.
- Continue to seek training in Christian development, as well as other training.
- Seek a mentor who has experience in Christian development.
- Read, study and become a lifelong learner.
- Be patient; this is a long and fruitful journey.
- Develop a passion for the ministry of development.

These are only a few ways to become a development leader in your organization. We must do more than attend one seminar and then try to change and shape our organizations. We must remain students and then become advocates and teachers, having patience and determination to achieve long-term results. Then we will have earned the right to be heard.

The board is next
The board is critical to the focus and philosophy of every organization. What is embraced at the top of the organization filters down eventually. This is true of accepting and endorsing the understanding of development as ministry.

The board is responsible for the mission and welfare of the organization. The board provides the leadership that staff and donors will follow. As development officers, we must communicate to the board how a development program with ministry as its foundation is more successful and honoring to God than merely a fund-raising program.

Consider starting with monthly development reports as part of the monthly board member packet. This packet could include the executive director's report, the latest financial statement, and updates on development programs. It would also include board committee reports and upcoming action items.

Share with them not only the financial implications of the development program but the people implications as well. Share a testimony or a letter from a donor. Share how donors were blessed by giving.

When given the opportunity, prepare a devotional or a training session for the board on biblical foundations for development. This might take place at the start of a monthly board meeting. Or it may be part of an annual board retreat.

As I do development audits in my consulting I always offer this training in development philosophy during my two-day consultation. Most times I will make a presentation to the board following the audit. It is interesting to see how many times the board feels it does not need training in biblical foundations in development. After spending time with them it usually is made clear that they have little or no understanding of the principles of relationship building or of how development is a part of God's plan for good stewardship. They want to know how the consultant or development officer can raise more money so "real" ministry can take place.

This doesn't surprise me. But when I explain the real ministry of development to a board, I am amazed at how quickly they grasp the concept and (usually) take immediate action. They want to raise more money, but they realize that honoring God and building relationships with donors is vital. Boards that take the time to study and reflect upon this subject make great strides for future growth in development. The Christian development officer can be the catalyst or agent of change to assist the board in grasping this vision.

Getting the CEO on board
While the board's understanding of development is important, the real change must take place in the partnership between the development officer and the CEO. The CEO is the chief fundraiser and must embrace any policy or philosophy.

The relationship between a CEO and the senior development officer is as varied as the combinations of job descriptions and responsibilities. In many ministries these positions are the same person.

When there are two different professionals in these roles, communication becomes critical. The relationship must be based on open and constant communication. The senior development officer's role is to create a ministry of development in which the CEO can go out and minister to donors. She or he will be very involved in implementing a philosophy of caring for donors, nurturing them and appreciating them. This can be difficult if the CEO is not comfortable with this philosophy or if he or she struggles with development in general. The best that can be hoped for in this case is a policy of non-interference where the development officer is able to create and implement a development program with a ministry focus.

The best-case scenario is where the two are a team of ministers who care for and encourage the donors to become an integral part of the ministry through giving, praying and serving. The organization with a team like this will find great success.

Train development staff

It does little good if the board and the CEO are expecting a development ministry but the development staff who is expected to implement the program has no understanding of what is to be done. We must keep training staff members to recognize and implement a ministry approach to our development projects and programs.

Begin with an annual retreat. Take a day away from the office and retreat to a place where there will be no interruptions. Fill your agenda with discussions of the biblical foundations and principles of a ministry of development. Then seek input from your staff as to how your current development programs can be more sensitive to the donors. Ask them how their efforts can become ministry rather than just income-producing programs.

Set up goals and calendars to implement the decisions you make that day. Realize this is a long-term project and cannot be accomplished overnight. Depending on the size of your organization and development staff, this can take one to three years to implement fully.

After the first retreat, plan quarterly informal meetings or lunches to check on progress. What has been implemented? What has not? Have the donors noticed? Have any non-development staff noticed?

Create training as a budget item for the entire staff. Sending everyone to distant conferences is not always possible, but local or regional conferences can be affordable.

Consider how a consultant can assist in training. Combine with other local ministries to bring in a consultant and share the costs. This can be cost-effective in that the staff are trained as a team rather than as individuals in seminars.

Minister to your development staff

Investing in development staff will be a ministry in and of itself. As they catch the vision for connecting donors to the ministry, and how it is part of God's plan, they will become more focused and hopefully more successful in their service.

A final point: do not assume that after this initial training that all development staff are on board. Continual sharing, training and encouragement are needed. As new staff members come on board they must be brought up to speed with current programs as well as biblical foundations. This could even be a part of the hiring process. Create a training and updating process that keeps staff informed of the ministry of development in the organization.

Educate donors

We cannot stand on a soapbox and preach stewardship and giving. It will come across as self-serving and manipulative.

But there are things we can do as educators to assist our donors in understanding their role and our role in the ministry of development.

First, we can create an open and honest program. The creation of guidelines for development, an annual report and audited financial statements are a good place to start. They can then be offered to donors through the newsletter or other communication avenues.

Next, how we write our appeals, newsletters and promotional materials will say a great deal about our philosophy. Are they hype or truth? Do we use effective, truthful stories or generalizations that play on emotions? These are tough issues without black-and-white answers, but our communications send a message and create an image in the mind of the donor as to who we are and what we stand for.

After a foundation of teaching and implementation has been established, a more advanced form of communication is possible. A development newsletter containing donor testimonies and their stewardship beliefs is a proven tool. I know of a well- written donor newsletter used for a Christian university foundation. It spotlights donors who created a trust or scholarship. The newsletter communicates their views as to why they gave. It educates other donors in the principles of stewardship and giving through the stories of their peers.

Finally, market research through surveys, mail and phone interviews can gather important information about your donors. It also lets them know the organization is listening. They will appreciate the fact that the ministry cares about what they think and feel. Knowing a ministry desires a relationship with them is a welcome and refreshing change from how some have operated in the past.

These are just a few ways to educate donors while also ministering to them. It is a sad fact that many churches are no longer effective in teaching biblical foundations for giving and stewardship. Entire generations of adults since the 1960's have lived outside the church and are now returning with no foundations in giving. They might not grasp their responsibilities for kingdom work if congregations are not providing the needed education. Ministries take up this slack and can easily do so through the ministry of development.

This educational process has been dropped in the laps of Christian development officers by default. We must step up and create an educational process where donors are taught, challenged and encouraged to become the stewards God has meant them to be.

Practice what you preach!

As a ministry of development is created and implemented there will be tough decisions. Which words will we use in the next appeal? How serious is our "crisis?" Does the board know what we are doing in development? Is this estate plan in the best interest of the donor even though the organization stands to receive the greatest gift in its history?

The ministry of development is not an easy path to follow. There will be many opportunities to use what works over what is best for the donor.

Do not settle for an average effort. The future of your organization is at stake. Work to build, grow and improve every area of development and the donors will respond. The results speak for themselves in other nonprofits (non-religious) where relationship building/marketing has already become a common philosophy.

We who have a higher calling in ministry should be on the cutting edge of implementing this process. We must practice what we preach to honor God and God's people while serving the mission and ministry.

Conclusion

Christian development professionals will find numerous challenges and pitfalls, but a great number of joys and rewards as well.

Organizations and individuals have many opportunities to grow. Organizations do well to remember that increasing knowledge for the individual will benefit the entire ministry.

I hope this collection of philosophy, theories and technical strategies challenge you to examine your motives as a development professional, and to examine the motives and strategies of the ministry you serve.

As research and knowledge in the field of Christian development expand, so will the quality and level of relationships with our donors. Everyone benefits from biblically based, quality programs. The final result is a strengthened ministry that shares the message of hope found in Jesus Christ.

And remember, God is honored in our efforts as we carry out the ministry of development.

The Christian Stewardship Association introduced this covenant for fund-raisers. I offer it as a starting point for anyone interested in using his/her personal gifts and abilities in the ministry of development.

Covenant for
Christian Fund-raisers

Acknowledging the Lordship of Jesus Christ and the need for dependence on him, I solemnly covenant before God and with other Christian fund-raisers to:

1. Ask the Lord to make my conscience sensitive to his leading in fund-raising decisions.

2. Search the scriptures diligently to discover the Lord's will in regard to fund-raising practices.

3. Bring before the Lord in prayer difficult fund-raising decisions.

4. Honor Christ by building up relationships between ourselves and those who are actively participating in our ministry.

May God help me through his Spirit, by his grace and for his glory to be faithful to this covenant. Amen.

Biblical Principles of
Stewardship and Fundraising

Compiled by Wesley K. Willmer (Vice President, University Advancement, Biola University) and the Committee on Evangelical Fundraising Guidelines as requested by the Evangelical Council for Financial Accountability

Christian leaders, including development staff, who believe in the Gospel of Jesus Christ and choose prayerfully to pursue eternal kingdom values (Mt. 6:19-21), will seek to identify the sacred kingdom resources of God's economy within these parameters:

1. God, the creator (Gen. 1) and sustainer of all things (Col. 1:17) and the One "who works within us to accomplish far more than we can ask or imagine," (Eph. 3:20), is a God of infinite abundance (Ps. 50:10-11) and grace (2 Cor. 9:8).

2. Acknowledging the primacy of the Gospel (Rom. 1:16) as our chief treasure (Mt. 13:44), Christians are called to lives of stewardship, as managers of all that God has entrusted to them (1 Cor. 4:1-2).

3. A Christian's attitude toward possessions on earth is important to God (Mt. 6:24), and there is a vital link between how believers utilize earthly possessions (as investments in God's kingdom) and the eternal rewards that believers receive (Phil. 4:17).

4. God entrusts possessions to Christians and holds them accountable for their use, as a tool to grow God's eternal kingdom, as a test of the believer's faithfulness to God, and as a trademark that their lives reflect Christ's values (Lk. 16:1-9).

5. From God's abounding grace, a Christian's giving reflects his gratitude for what God has provided and involves growing in one's intimate faith relationship with Christ as Lord of their lives (Mk. 12:21-22).

6. Because giving is a worshipful, obedient act of returning to God from what has been provided (1 Chron. 29:10-14), Christian fundraisers should hold a conviction that, in partnership with the church, they have an important role in the spiritual maturation of believers (James 3:1).

7. The primary role of Christian fundraisers is to advance and facilitate a believer's faith in and worship of God through a Christ-centered understanding of stewardship that is solidly grounded on Scripture (2 Tim. 3:16).

8. Recognizing it is the work of the Holy Spirit that prompts Christians to give (Jn. 15:4-5)-often in partnership with fundraising techniques (2 Cor. 9:5-7, Neh. 1:4-11), fundraisers and/or organizations must never manipulate or violate their sacred trust with ministry partners.

9. An eternal, God-centered worldview promotes cooperation, rather than competition, among organizations, and places the giver's relationship to God above the ministry's agenda (2 Cor. 4:16-18).

10. In our materialistic, self-centered culture, Christian leaders should acknowledge that there is a great deal of unclear thinking about possessions, even among believers, and that an eternal kingdom perspective will often seem like foolish nonsense (1 Cor. 2:14) to those who rely on earthly kingdom worldview techniques (1 Cor. 2:1-5).

When these principles are implemented, that rely on God changing hearts more than on human methods, the resulting joy-filled generosity of believers will fully fund God's work here on earth (Ex. 36:6-7).

SECTION FOUR

RESOURCES

BIBLIOGRAPHY

AAFRC Trust for Philanthropy. *Giving USA 2004, Report on Philanthropy for 2003*. Indianapolis, IN: Giving USA Foundation, 2004.

AFP Ethics Committee, "Ethics Report." *Advancing Philanthropy*, March/April 2006, 4.

Alcorn, Randy. *Money, Possessions, and Eternity*. Carol Stream, IL: Tyndale, 2003.

_____. *The Treasure Principle: Discovering the Secret of Joyful Giving*. Sisters, OR: Multnomah, 2001.

American Association of Fundraising Counsel. *Home Page*. Giving U.S.A. http://www.aafrc.org (accessed September 1, 2005).

Andringa, Robert C., and Ted W. Engstrom. *Nonprofit Board Answer Book*. 2nd ed. Washington, D.C.: Board-Source, 2002.

Apostolic Council for Educational Accountability. *Home Page*. Global Harvest Ministries. http://www.acea-schools.org (accessed February 1, 2007).

Association of Fundraising Professionals, *About AFP*. Association of Fundraising Professionals, http://www.nsfre.org/about_afp (accessed February 28, 2007).

Association of Fundraising Professionals. *Home Page.* AFP. http://www.nsfre.org (accessed March 15, 2006).

Association of Fundraising Professionals. *Jobs.* http://www.jobs/afpnet.org (accessed January 18, 2008).

Association of Theological Schools. *Welcome.* ATS. http://www.ats.edu (accessed February 4, 2007).

Banks, Robert. Re-envisioning Theological Education: Exploring a Missional Alternative to Current Models. Grand Rapids, MI: William B. Eerdmans, 1999.

Barna, George. *The Barna Update 2002.* The Barna Group. http://www.barna.org (accessed October 2006).

_____. *Churches Lose Financial Ground in 2000.* The Barna Group, http://www.barna.org, (accessed October 1, 2006)

_____. How to Increase Giving in Your Local Church. Ventura. CA: Regal, 1997.

_____. *Revolution.* Wheaton, IL: Tyndale, 2005.

_____. Survey Shows Pastors Claim Congregants are Deeply Committed to God but Congregants Deny It. The Barna Report, http://www.Barna.org (accessed November 28, 2007).

The Barna Group. *Giving to Churches Rose Substantially in 2003.* The Barna Update. April 13, 2004. http://www.barna.org/ (accessed August 28, 2007).

_____. *Home Page.* The Barna Group. http://www.barna.org (accessed September 1, 2005).

_____. *New Study Shows Trends in Tithing and Donating.* The Barna Update. April 14, 2008. http://www. barna.org/FlexPage.aspx?Page=BarnaUpdateNarrow Preview&BarnaUpdateID=296 (accessed July 3, 2008).

_____. *Tithing Down 62% in the Past Year.* The Barna Update. May 19, 2003. http://www.barna.org/FlexPage. aspx?Page=BarnaUpdate&BarnaUpdateID=139 (accessed September 15, 2007)..

Block, Peter. *Stewardship: Choosing Service over Self-Interest.* San Francisco: Berrett-Koehler, 1993.

Blomberg, Craig L. Heart, Soul, and Money: A Christian View of Possessions. Joplin, MO: College Press, 2000.

_____. Neither Poverty nor Riches: A Biblical Theology of Material Possessions. Grand Rapids, MI: William B. Eerdmans, 1999.

BoardSource. *Home Page.* Boardsource. http://www.board source.org (accessed February 1, 2006).

Boice, Jacklyn P. *Getting Down to Business.* Advancing Philanthropy. May, 2005, 16.

_____. What's Your Plan? Advancing Philanthropy. January/February 2005, 28.

Boulding, William. *Leadership Development in the Duke Day MBA Program.* Leader to Leader, no. Special Supplement (2007): 47-52.

Bremner, Robert H. *Giving.* New Brunswick, NJ: Transaction, 1994.

Burnett, Ken. *Relationship Fundraising.* 2nd ed. San Francisco: Jossey-Bass, 2002.

Callahan, Kennon L. Giving and Stewardship in an Effective Church: A Guide for Every Member. San Francisco: Jossey-Bass, 1997.

Campbell, Bruce. *Listening to Your Donors*. San Francisco: Jossey-Bass, 2000.

Center on Philanthropy at Indiana University. *Home*. Indiana University Purdue University Indianapolis. http:// www.philanthropy.iupui.edu/Education/ma.aspx (accessed July 3, 2008).

Champlin, Joseph M. Grateful Caretakers of God's Many Gifts: A Parish Manual to Foster the Sharing of Time, Talent, and Treasure. Collegeville, MN: Liturgical Press, 2002.

_____. A Way of Life: Four Faith-Sharing Sessions About Sacrificial Giving, Stewardship, and Grateful Caretaking. Collegeville, MN: Liturgical Press, 2004.

Christian and Missionary Alliance. *Theology of Stewardship: An Executive Summary*. Christian and Missionary Alliance. http://www.cmalliance.org/search/ ?query= Theology%20of%20Stewardship (accessed August 15, 2006).

Christian Community Foundation. *Home*. Water Stone. http://www.thefoundations.org (accessed March 15, 2006).

_____. *Biblical Principles of Stewardship and Fundraising*. Christian Stewardship Association. http://www.stewardship.org/resources/Fund_Articles/ principles-fundraising.html (accessed September 1, 2005).

_____. *2007 Steward Leadership Institute: Development*. Christian Stewardship Association. http://www.steward ship.org/events/Institute/ 2007/index_old.html (accessed January 18, 2008).

The Chronicle of Philanthropy. *Home.* The Chronicle of Philanthropy. http://www.philanthropy.com (accessed February 15, 2006).

Clemenson, Barbara. *Stewardship in Nonprofit Organizations, Part 1.* Charity Channel. March 2, 2006. http://www.CharityChannel.com (accessed April 1, 2006).

————. *Stewardship in Nonprofit Organizations, Part 2.* Charity Channel. March 17, 2006. http://www.CharityChannel.com (accessed June 1, 2006).

Commission on Stewardship and Development. *Report to the General Convention.* Episcopal Church Report. 2005, 279-383.

Council for Advancement and Support of Education. *Home.* CASE. http://www.case.org (accessed March 1, 2006).

Crown Financial Ministries. *Home.* Crown Financial Ministries. http://www.crown.org (accessed November 1, 2005).

Davis, C. Neal. *Ask and Ye Shall Receive.* Advancing Philanthropy. September/October, 2005, 38.

Delloff, Linda Marie. (2006). *Beyond Stewardship: A Theology of Nature.* The Lutheran. http://www.webofcreation.org/Manuals/krause/foreword.html (accessed October 15, 2006).

Dick, Dan R. Revolutionizing Christian Stewardship for the 21st Century: Lessons from Copernicus. Nashville, TN: Discipleship Resources, 1997.

Dingman, Bruce. *The Difficult Search for a Chief Development Officer.* Reflections from the Lamp. Winter 2007. http://www.dingman.com/newsletters/ NEWS_Winter07.htm (accessed November 15, 2007).

Dove, Kent E. *Conducting a Successful Capital Campaign.* San Francisco: Jossey-Bass, 1988.

Doudera, Ralph. *Wealth Conundrum.* Atlanta, GA: Christian Wealth, 2005.

Durall, Michael. Creating Congregations of Generous People: Money, Faith, and Lifestyle Series. Herndon, VA: The Alban Institute, 1999.

Duranio, Margaret A., and Eugene R. Tempel. *Fund Raisers: Their Careers, Stories, Concerns, and Accomplishments.* San Francisco: Jossey-Bass, 1997.

Ecumenical Stewardship Center. *Home.* Ecumenical Stewardship Center. http://www.stewardshipresources.org (accessed October 1, 2006).

Edles, L. Peter. Fundraising: Hands on Tactics for Nonprofit Groups. New York: McGraw Hill, 1993.

Episcopal Church of the Resurrection. *Home.* Episcopal Church of the Resurrection. http://www.resurrection church.com (accessed October 1, 2006).

Episcopal Diocese of Western Massachusetts. *Home Page-Welcome.* Episcopal Diocese of Western Massachusetts. http://www.diocesewma.org (accessed October 15, 2006).

Eternal Perspective Ministries. *Home.* Eternal Perspective Ministries. http://www.epm.org (accessed November 1, 2006).

Evangelical Council for Financial Accountability. *Home.* ECFA. http://www.ecfa.org (accessed September 20, 2005).

Flanagan, Joan. *Successful Fundraising.* Chicago: Contemporary, 1991.

Frank, John R. The Monthly Partner: Discovering the Missing Jewel in your Donors. Steward Publishing, 2003.

Generous Giving. *Home.* Generous Giving. http://www. generousgiving.org (accessed September 15, 2005).

Generous Giving. *Statistics and Trends: Giving Among Denominations.* http:// www.generousgiving.org/page. asp?sec=4&page=161 (accessed July 3, 2008).

Getz, Gene A. *A Biblical Theology of Material Possessions.* Chicago: Moody Press, 1990.

_____. Real Prosperity: Biblical Principles and Material Possessions. Chicago: Moody Press, 1990.

Giving USA Foundation. *Giving USA (The Annual Report on Philanthropy for the Year 2006).* Quoted in "Current Research," Center on Philanthropy at Indiana University, Lake Institute. http://www.philanthropy.iupui.edu/ Lake-FamilyInstitute/current_research.aspx (accessed July 3, 2008).

The Good Steward. *Home.* The Good Steward. http://www. thegoodsteward.com (accessed October 1, 2006).

Gordon, David W. A Plan for Stewardship Education and Development through the Year. 3rd ed. Harrisburg, PA: Morehouse, 1998.

Grimm, Eugene. *Generous People.* Edited by Herb Miller. Nashville, TN: Abingdon Press, 1992.

Grissen, Lillian V. *Firstfruits: Managing the Master's Money*. 2nd ed. Orland Park, IL: Barnabas Foundation, 1992.

Grizzard, Chip. *A Stewardship Model of Fundraising*. Christian Management Report. February, 2003, 10

Guinness, Os. *Doing Well and Doing Good*. Colorado Springs: NavPress, 2001.

Hall, Chad. Missional: Possible—Steps to Transform a Consumer Church into a Missional Church. Leadership Journal 28, no.1 (Winter 2007): 34-37.

Hall, Douglas John. *The Steward: A Biblical Symbol Come of Age*. Grand Rapids, MI: William B. Eerdmans, 1990.

Hall, Holly. *Fund Raisers: In Demand, in the Money*. The Chronicle of Philanthropy. February 10, 2000. http://www.philanthropy.com/free/articles/v12/i08/08002301.htm (accessed November 20, 2007).

_____. Raising Funds by the Good Book: Churches Use Financial Lessons from the Bible and See Gifts Rise. The Chronicle of Philanthropy. June 17, 1999.

Hoag, Gary. *ATS Peer Group Advancement Study*. In Development and Institutional Advancement-ATS. edited by Gary Hoag, 1-4. Orlando, FL: ATS, 2007.

Holland, Thomas P., and David C. Hester. *Building Effective Boards for Religious Organizations*. San Francisco: Jossey-Bass, 1999.

Hughes, Selwyn. *Divine Mathematics, How One Plus One Equals Three in the Kingdom*. Vol. 1. Chattanooga, TN: Generous Giving, 2003.

Hybels, Bill. *The Volunteer Revolution*. Grand Rapids, MI: Zondervan, 2004.

Indiana University-Purdue University Indianapolis. *The Center for Philanthropy at Indiana University.* http://www. philanthropy.iupui.edu (accessed March 15, 2006).

Jeavons, Thomas H., and Rebekah Burch Basinger. *Growing Givers' Hearts: Treating Fundraising as a Ministry.* San Francisco: Jossey-Bass, 2000.

Jones, L. Gregory, and Stephanie Paulsell. *The Scope of Our Art: The Vocation of the Theological Teacher.* Grand Rapids, MI: William B. Eerdmans, 2002.

Jones, Tony. *Thoughts on Organization.* Emergent/C: eNewsletter. Kansas City, MO, www.emergentvillage. com (accessed September 12, 2006).

Keegan, P. Burke. Fundraising for Non-Profits: How to Build a Community Partnership. New York: HarperCollins, 1990.

Kelly, Russell Earl. *Should the Church Teach Tithing?* New York: Writers Club Press, 2000.

Kluth, Brian. *Biblical Resources and Speaking Ministry to Increase Giving.* Maximum Generosity, http:// kluth.org/specificpage (accessed April, 10, 2007).

———. *Maximum Generosity: Home Page.* Maximum Generosity. http://www.kluth.org/ (accessed September 15, 2006).

LaCugna, Catherine M. *God for Us: The Trinity and the Christian Life.* San Francisco: Harpers, 1993.

Lant, Jeffrey L. Development Today: A Fund Raising Guide for Nonprofit Organizations. 5th ed. Cambridge, MA: JLA, 1993.

Lawson, Douglas M. *Give to Live: How Giving Can Change Your Life*. La Jolla, CA: ALTI, 1991.

Levan, Christopher. Living in the Maybe: A Steward Confronts the Spirit of Fundamentalism. Grand Rapids, MI: William B. Eerdmans, 1998.

The Living Pulpit. *Home*. The Living Pulpit. http://www.pulpit.org (accessed October 14, 2006).

The Lutheran Church-Missouri Synod, *Congregational Stewardship Workbook*. St. Louis, MO: The Lutheran Church-Missouri Synod, 2000.

MacDonald, Gordon. *Secrets of the Generous Life*. Wheaton, IL: Tyndale, 2002.

_____. *Generosity, moving toward life that is truly life*. Alpharetta, GA, National Christian Foundation, 2009

McGrath, Alister E. Historical Theology: An Introduction to the History of Christian Thought. Malden, MA: Blackwell, 1998.

McLaughlin, Patrick G. Major Donor Game Plan, The Timothy Group, Grand Rapids, MI. 2006.

McLeish, Barry J. The Donor Bond: How to Nurture Your Donors Using Strategic Marketing and Management Techniques. Rockville, MD: Fund Raising Institute, 1991.

_____. Successful Marketing Strategies for Nonprofit Organizations. New York: Wiley and Sons, 1995.

McNamara, Patrick H. *Called to Be Stewards: Bringing New Life to Catholic Parishes*. Collegeville, MN: Liturgical Press, 2003.

_____. *More Than Money: Portraits of Transformative Stewardship*. Edited by M. Douglas Meeks. Bethesda, MD: Alban Institute, 1999.

Mercer, Joyce Ann. Teaching the Bible in Congregations: A Congregational Studies Pedagogy for Contextual Education. Religious Education 2 (2005): 1-3.

Michael, S. H. *We're in the Money!* Christianity Today 44 no. 7 (2000): 36.

Miller, Herb. Full Disclosure: Everything the Bible Says About Financial Giving. Nashville, TN: Discipleship Resources, 2003.

Mills, James. *Contributing to a Conversation*. Emergent/C: eNewsletter. Kansas City, MO, www.emergentvillage.com (accessed January 25, 2007).

Money for Ministry. *Home*. Money for Ministry. http://www.moneyforministry.com (accessed February 1, 2006).

Moore, Gary. *Please Live Responsibly*. In Development and Institutional Advancement-ATS, edited by Gary Moore, 1-12 Orlando, FL: The Financial Seminary, 2007.

New York University, School of Continuing and Professional Studies. *Heyman Center for Philanthropy and Fundraising: MS in Fundraising*. New York University. http://www.scps.nyu.edu/areas-of-study/philanthropy-fundraising/graduate-programs/ms-fundraising/index.html (accessed November 20, 2007).

Nichols, Judith. Pinpointing Affluence: Increasing Your Share of Major Donor Dollars. Chicago: Precept Press, 1994.

_____. Targeted Fund Raising: Defining and Redefining Your Development Strategy. Chicago: Precept Press, 1991.

The NonProfit Times. *Home Page*. The NonProfit Times. http://www.nptimes.com (accessed January 15, 2006).

North, Gary. *Tithing and the Church*. Tyler, TX: Institute for Christian Economics, 1994.

O'Hurley-Pitts, Michael. The Passionate Steward: Recovering Christian Stewardship from Secular Fundraising. Toronto: St. Brigid Press, 2002.

Ortberg, John, Laurie Pederson, and Judson Poling. *Giving: Unlocking the Heart of Good Stewardship*. Grand Rapids, MI: Zondervan, 2000.

Oster, Merrill J., and Mike Hamel. *Giving Back: Using Your Influence to Create Social Change*. Colorado Springs: NavPress, 2003.

Panas, Jerold. *Mega Gifts*. Chicago: Pluribus Press, 1984.

Parker, Terry A., Gregory L. Sperry, and David H. Wills. *Investing in God's Business: The "How To" of Smart Christian Business*. Atlanta, GA: National Christian Foundation, 2005.
Perkins, John, H. *Practical Theology: What Will it Become*. Christian Century February 1-8, 1984.

Piper, John. *Money: The Currency of Christian Hedonism*. Vol. 1. Chattanooga, TN: Generous Giving, 2003.

Presbyterian Church USA. *Living Grateful Lives: Stewardship Theology in Our Time*. Presbyterian Church USA http://www.secondpres.info/about2pc/Stewardship.htm (accessed October 14, 2006).

Proffit, Brian. *How Churches are Ending Passivity in the Pews*. Christian Management Report (2005): 11-12.

Ramp, Stephen. *Carnal Giving vs. Biblical Stewardship*. The Clergy Journal (2003): 15-16.

Reid, David R. *Stewardship Theology*. The Living Pulpit (July-September 2006). http://www.pulpit.org/articles/StewardshipTheology.asp (accessed November 4, 2006).

Reumann, John. *Stewardship and the Economy of God*. Grand Rapids, MI: William B. Eerdmans, 1992.

Richards, Robert. *The Economics Underlying Stewardship: Creation and Distribution of Wealth*, Luther Seminary Stewardship Resource Database, http:// www.luthersem.edu/stewardship/resource_detail.asp?resource_id=974 (accessed November 28, 2007).

Rockwell, Bruce. *Parish Stewardship Program: My Theology of Stewardship*. Episcopal Diocese of Western Massachusetts. http://www.diocesewma.org/ resources/parishstew.html (accessed November 15, 2006).

Rodin, R. Scott. *Revolution in Generosity*. Wes Willmer, ed. Chicago: Moody Press, 2008.

_____. Stewards in the Kingdom: A Theology of Life in All Its Fullness. Downers Grove, IL: InterVarsity Press, 2000.

Roost, Charles. *Taking Hold of Life*. Steward to Steward (Winter 2007): 2.

_____, and Ben Ingebretson. *All the Gold Is Mine*. Growing in the Grace of Giving Foundational Papers, no. 2. Grand Rapids, MI: International Steward for the Freedom Foundation, 2003.

Rosso, Henry A. Achieving Excellence in Fund Raising: A Comprehensive Guide to Principles, Strategies, and Methods. San Francisco: Jossey-Bass, 1991.

Roush, Christine. *Swimming Upstream: Reflections on Consumerism and Culture.* Kohler, WI: Design Group International, 2009.

Saint Mary's University of Minnesota. *MA Philanthropy and Development.* Saint Mary's University of Minnesota. http://www.smumn.edu/sitepages/pid585.php (accessed March 15, 2006).

Sargeant, Adrian, and Elaine Jay. *Building Donor Loyalty: The Fundraiser's Guide to Increasing Lifetime Value.* San Francisco: Jossey-Bass, 2004.

_____. *Fundraising Management: Analysis, Planning and Practice.* New York: Routledge, 2004.

Saul, Jason. *Benchmarking for Nonprofits: How to Measure, Manage, and Improve Performance.* Saint Paul, MN: Wilder Foundation, 2004.

Schoenhals, G. Roger. *On My Way in Planned Giving: Inspiring Anecdotes and Advice for Gift-Planning Professionals.* Seattle: Planned Giving Today, 1995.

_____. *Why Focus on Bequests? Planned Giving Mentor,* April 2006.

Schwarzentraub, Betsy. *Afire with God: Becoming Spirited Stewards.* Nashville, TN: Discipleship Resources, 2000.

Smith, Wendell, and Oral Roberts. *Prosperity with a Purpose.* Kirkland, WA: The City Church Press, 2005.

Stanley, Andy. *Fields of Gold.* Carol Stream, IL: Tyndale, 2004.

_____. *Sowing Seeds of Generosity, Message Given at Generous Giving Conference*. Generous Giving. http://www.generousgiving.org (accessed September 19, 2006).

Stott, John R.W. *Generous Giving*. Generous Giving 1, no. 15 (2003): 1.

Strait, C. Neal. *Stewardship Is More Than Time, Talent, and Things*. Kansas City, MO: Beacon Hill Press, 1993.

Sweet, Leonard. ed. *The Church in Emerging Culture: Five Perspectives*. Grand Rapids, MI: Zondervan, 2003.

_____. *Freely You Have Received, Freely Give*. Sweetened: Articles and Writings (2005). http://www.leonardsweet.com/includes/ShowSweetenedArticles.asp?articleID=91http:// (accessed October 16, 2005).

Tamasy, Robert J. *The Handout, Andy Stanley Gave It Away*. Life@Work 3, no. 3 (2000): 48

Taylor, C. W. *Stewardship is the Main Work of the Church*. Episcopal Church of the Resurrection. http://www.resurrectionchurch.com/resources/stewardship.html (accessed August 15, 2006).

Tierney, Thomas J. *Understanding the Nonprofit Sector's Leadership Deficit*. Leader to Leader. Special Supplement (2006): p. 13-19.

_____. *The Leadership Deficit*. Stanford Social Innovation Review. Summer 2006, 29.

Towner, Dick. *10 Questions for Dick Towner of Willow Creek Association*. Christian Stewardship Association, http://www.stewardship.org/resources/Fund_Articles/towner_art.html (accessed May 30, 2007).

_____. *More Good $ense: November 2006*. Willow Creek Association. www.goodsenseministry.com/ newsletter (accessed October 2006).

United States Conference of Catholic Bishops, Ad Hoc Committee on Stewardship. *Stewardship: A Disciple's Response: A Pastoral Letter on Stewardship*. Washington, D.C.: Conference of Catholic Bishops, 2002.

Van Engen, Charles. *Shifting Paradigms in Ministry Formation*. Glendora, CA: Fuller Press, 1994.

Van Til, John. *Critical Issues in American Philanthropy: Strengthening Theory and Practice*. San Francisco: Jossey-Bass, 1990.

Vincent, Mark L. *A Christian View of Money: Celebrating God's Generosity, 3rd ed*. Eugene, OR: Wipf & Stock, 2007.

_____. *A Stewardship Manifest*. Kohler, WI: Design Group Publishing: 1999.

_____. *Speaking About Money: Reducing the Tension*. Scottdale, PA: Herald Press, 2001.

Warren, Rick. *Biblical Generosity, Message Given at Generous Giving Conference*. Generous Giving. http://www.generousgiving.org (accessed August 15, 2006).

Watley, William D. *Bring the Full Tithe: Sermons on the Grace of Giving*. Valley Forge, PA: Judson Press, 1995.

Web of Creation. *Home*. Web of Creation. http://www.webofcreation.org (accessed October 2, 2006).

Weiss, Daniel. *The History of Economic Dependence: The Need to Rethink Prevailing Approaches to Missions*. International Steward (2005): 1-2.

Wiersbe, Warren W. *Classic Sermons on Stewardship*. Grand Rapids, MI: Kregel, 1999.

Wilkinson, Bruce. *A Life God Rewards: Why Everything You Do Today Matters Forever*. Sisters, OR: Multnomah, 2002.

Willard, Dallas. *Renovation of the Heart: Putting on the Character of Christ*. Colorado Springs: NavPress, 2002.

Willmer, Wesley K., ed. *Revolution in Generosity: Transforming Stewards to Be Rich Toward God*. Chicago, IL, Moody, 2008.

Willmer, Wesley K., J. David Schmidt, and Martyn Smith. *The Prospering Parachurch: Enlarging the Boundaries of God's Kingdom*. San Francisco: Jossey-Bass, 1998.

Willmer, Wesley K., and Martyn Smith. *God and Your Stuff: The Vital Link between Your Possessions and Your Soul*. Colorado Springs: NavPress, 2002.

World Vision. *You're Invited to Join Us at the National Pastors Convention in San Diego, Feb 22-25*. World Vision eNews. http://www.worldvision.org/ about_us.nsf/child/ eNews_pastors_100405?OpenDocument&lid=1005past orsconv&lpos=main (accessed November 20, 2007).

Wuthnow, Robert, and Virginia A. Hodgkinson. *Faith and Philanthropy in America: Exploring the Role of Religion in America's Voluntary Sector*. San Francisco: Jossey-Bass, 1990.

Organizations

Association of Fundraising Professionals
www.afp.org

CASE (Council for Advancement and Support of Education)
www.case.org

CLA (Christian Leadership Alliance)
www.ChristianLeadershipAlliance.org

Christian Stewardship Network
www.ChristianStewardshipNetwork.org

The Foundation Center
www.foundationcenter.org

The Grantsmanship Center
www.tcgi.com

Institute for Charitable Giving
www.instituteforgiving.org

Association of Gospel Rescue Missions
www.agrm.org

ChristianCampandConferenceAssociation.org
www.ccca.org

Evangelical Council for Financial Accountability
www.ecfa.org

Care Net
www.care-net.org

Creation Care
www.creationcare.org

Training Materials

Chronicle of Philanthropy
P.O. Box 1989
Marion, OH 43306
www.philanthropy.com

The Frank Group
www.TheFrankGroup.us

Design Group International™
www.DesignGroupInternational.com

Generous Giving
www.generousgiving.org

Training Programs

Christian Leadership Alliance
The Certified Stewardship Professional
www.ChristianLeadershipAlliance.org

Saint Mary's University of Minnesota
Winona, Minnesota
M.A. in Philanthropy and Development   (507) 457-7000
www.smumn.edu/Philanthropy.aspx

Indiana Center for Philanthropic Studies
Indianapolis, Indiana
Various programs, certificates, degrees   (317) 274-4200
www.philanthropy.iupui.edu

Southwestern Baptist Seminary
Center for Stewardship Studies
www.swbts.edu

Lake Institute on Faith and Giving
www.philanthropy.iupui.edu/LakeFamilyInstitute

International Steward
Grand Rapids, MI
www.internationalsteward.org

About the Author

Dr. John R. Frank, CFRE
Speaker – Trainer - Author

John Frank is passionate about stewardship. He studies, teaches, and consults on stewardship and believes it is the key to a holistic approach to life for individuals and organizations.

A nationally and internationally recognized speaker and teacher, John's expertise includes stewardship, leadership, nonprofit organizations, as well as biblical training in various topics. He speaks with churches, ministry leadership, boards, and retreats.

His life experience includes ministry in 23 countries, pastor of worship, teaching stewardship in third world countries, evangelistic outreach behind the Iron Curtain, as well as church leadership. He consults with and provides training for many ministries ranging from start-ups to those with $100 million annual budgets.

He has authored numerous articles on stewardship, development and leadership. His second book, *The Monthly Partner* was published in 2005. He was also a contributing author to *Revolution in Generosity* as well as having contributed to *From Soup & a Sermon to Mega-Mission, A Guide to Financing Rescue Missions.*

To Contact Dr. John R. Frank, CFRE
JohnRFrank@TheFrankGroup.us
www.TheFrankGroup.us

Comments on John R. Frank's
The Ministry of Development

"It came to me as wonderful news that the book, <u>The Ministry of Development</u>, was being revised and re-released to the Christian resource development, finance, and stewardship world of professionals. I have encouraged John since the book's original inception of concept and original first edition writing. My advocacy for this opinion-led and biblically-based book is simple. I do not believe anyone should serve in Christian resource raising service without first becoming a student of this book's contents. This highly valuable book should be immediate and required reading by every person who purposes themselves to serve in Christian resource and development/advancement work. To stay in service, you need to know your groundings – your philosophical base for what you do. Most Christians who so wonderfully serve in the development community have never taken the time to reflect. . . the pause to consider why they do what they do in this unique calling to raise funds and friends. This book in my mind and opinion has stood in that gap in the Christian literature base. The information John Frank purposes here is inspiring, and purposed for the retention and growth of professionals who want to serve this way.

Whether you serve in stewardship in parachurch, or church, or independent ministry; international or unique to the Americas, you must commit yourself to an understanding of what John Frank encourages here. Ensure each development staffer whether opening envelopes or meeting donors one on one, reads, moreover has an ability to dialogue their own understanding of this book. You will be so blessed that you have done so yourself.

Scott
Scott Preissler, Ph.D.
Eklund Professor of Stewardship
Director: The Center for Biblical Stewardship
Department of Stewardship - School of Theology
Southwestern Baptist Theological Seminary

"There is a revolution in generosity taking place in the Church around the world. Christian leaders are realizing they must move beyond seeking to raise up gifts for the ministry they serve; they must raise up stewards to be rich toward God. To accomplish this Kingdom objective, Christian leaders need strategic *and* spiritual counsel. This book contains both. Don't just be a reader of this book. Do what it says!"

Gary Hoag, Generosity Monk

John Frank's book gave me a solid Biblical foundation for a lifetime in donor development. John helps ministry leaders and development representatives understand donor development as spiritual ministry to the people of God. When this concept of ministry is embraced and practiced, development activities each day will be filled with joy and eternal purpose. When growing Biblical stewards becomes our priority in ministry, funding for God's work will become a joyful by-product.

Doug M. Carter
Senior Vice President
EQUIP

Original Published Comments on John R. Frank's *The Ministry of Development* (1995)

John Frank's *Ministry of Development* provides an insightful overview of the basics of raising money from a biblical world view perspective and should prove helpful to those concerned with advancing Christian non-profits.

Dr. Wesley K. Willmer
Former Vice-President, University Advancement
Biola University

John has laid a foundation for a biblical philosophy of stewardship and demonstrated its application for entry level people or those new to development who will be involved in fund development. I found the Guidelines for Development especially helpful for the start-up development office.

Mark S. McCampbell, CFRE
Vice President Advancement
CRISTA Ministries

John Frank's book is a <u>must read</u> for any Christian leader who wants to fund their ministry according to solid biblical and development principles.

Brian Kluth
President
Christian Stewardship Association

Development is more than fund raising, and John Frank lives that fact as he has worked with RESCUE missions and other not for profit ministries. His book, *The Ministry of Development* is a guidebook to the Christian perspective. In these muddled times, a guidebook on God's Word is a great help. *The Ministry of Development* puts the proper face on fund raising for Christian Ministries.

Rev. Stephen E. Burger
Executive Director
International Union of Gospel Missions

Ministries can be funded the world's way or God's way. John Frank has done a major-league job of showing the wisdom and way of doing it God's way. It's must reading for everyone who is serious about doing God's work in God's way!

Dr. Bob Moorehead
Pastor
Overlake Christian Church, Kirkland, WA

John Frank writes not only theoretically — and well indeed — but also experientially related to the important ministry of Christian development. He is both an effective teacher and a practitioner in what is both a science and an art. I am happy to highly commend this book.

Dr. Ted W. Engstrom
President Emeritus
World Vision

LaVergne, TN USA
18 October 2010
201332LV00001B/6/P